Summer Activities

For grades 6-7

200 Fun, Fast-Paced Things to Do to Keep Your Brain From Turning to Mush on Your Summer Vacation

Marc Tyler Nobleman

KAPLAN

Published by Simon & Schuster

NEW YORK   LONDON   TORONTO   SYDNEY

Kaplan Publishing
Published by Simon & Schuster, Inc.
1230 Avenue of the Americas
New York, NY 10020

 A QUIRK PACKAGING BOOK

Illustrations on cover and page 36, 42, 67, 96, 150, 283,
197, 209, and 210 by Binny Hobbs
Illustrations on page 8, 24, 45, 55, 99, 105, 116, 142,
158, 159, and 231 by Nancy Leonard
Illustration on page 50 © National Organic Program

Manufactured in China

April 2006
10 9 8 7 6 5 4 3 2 1

ISBN-13: 978-0-7432-8625-1
ISBN-10: 0-7432-8625-1

For information regarding special discounts for
bulk purchases, please contact Simon & Schuster
Special Sales at 1-800-456-6798 or
business@simonandschuster.com.

Contents

To the
boys and girls
of summer.

Introduction

School's out for summer—yippee! You worked hard all year; now it's time to kick back and chill out, let that brain get some rest. On the other hand, you've heard the expression, "Use it or lose it," right? Hmmm. It would be kind of a shame if you forgot everything you worked so hard to learn. What if you try a few little activities to keep your brain cells from turning to mush? It could even be kind of fun.

That's what this book is for—a selection of fun things to do that will keep those skills and facts you learned during the school year from totally slipping your mind. Don't fear—these activities are not like homework. But each activity is designed to reinforce a concept that you have encountered in **writing, reading, social studies, science,** or **math** class.

Some activities can be done on your own, while others are best done with a friend or sibling, or, if you can gather them together, a big group of participants. If you want, you could even include your parents in some of these games and activities—that is, if your folks are up for the challenge. Speaking of challenges, here's one: try to do as many of these activities as possible before the end of summer vacation. You can use the Subject Checklist at the back of the book (page 237) to mark each one off as you complete it.

Smart teachers know that there's nothing wrong with having fun during the school year. And smart kids know that there's also nothing wrong with learning during summer vacation!

The Activities

Social Studies   **Science**   **Writing**   **Reading**   **Math**

1. One Hundred Days of Summer

It may always seem like the summer goes too fast, but you actually have lots of time to do lots of things.

Keep track of how many days during the summer you enjoy these 3 popular vacation pastimes: read, see a movie, and play sports. Make 3 grids, each 10-by-10 squares, in other words, with 100 squares, for each of the 3 activities; the 100 squares represent 100 days of summer—June 1 through September 8. (Okay, summer officially starts and ends on June 21 and September 21, respectively, but that totals only 93 days, so we adjusted it based on weather, not the calendar.) Date each box in each grid and shade in the appropriate box for each day you do any of the activities. (You can see part of a sample reading grid at right.

At the end of summer, calculate what percentage of the summer you spent doing each activity. When you see how much you packed in, you may realize that summer didn't go so fast after all.

READING									
6/1	6/2	6/3	6/4	6/5	6/6	6/7	6/8	6/9	6/10
6/11	6/12	6/13	6/14	6/15	6/16	6/17	6/18	6/19	6/20
6/21	6/22	6/23	6/24	6/25	6/26	6/27	6/28	6/29	6/30

2. Protect Your Own Ecosystem

Ecosystems aren't all exotic and far away.

In fact, you're in an ecosystem right now. And just look at the shape it's in. Show some pride!

Recruit friends and an adult or two, pack a lunch, bring a radio and rubber gloves, and have fun improving your environment by cleaning up a nearby area. Choose someplace safe but in need of assistance—for example, a park that is strewn with litter or even your block. Photograph your site before and after you clean it to document the improvement. At the end of the day, whoever has filled the greatest number of garbage bags is the Clean Champion. And don't do this project just once; do it whenever you see trash where it doesn't belong.

3. Form a Secret Society of Readers

Once a week, head out in the darkness with a small item tucked under your arm.

Only your driver (that is, Mom or Dad) and the elite and secret group you are a part of will know your destination. Once all members have arrived at that week's top-secret location, the meeting of the Secret Society of Book Readers (SSBR) will begin. It's not a secret because you want to hide the fact that you like to read—you should be proud of that. What's secret are the discussions you and your friends—uh, the society members—will have about the book you are all currently reading. As a group, you'll choose a book to read, and you'll discuss it with no limits at your weekly meetings. Everyone must agree to read a certain portion by each meeting—for example, the first four chapters by the first meeting. And everyone takes turns choosing the next book the SSBR will read and discuss.

Add to the intrigue by having all SSBR members give themselves code names that everyone else must use during gatherings—but they must be book-related, of course. You might call yourself "Fowl" after the lead character in the Artemis Fowl series, and a friend could be "Dewey" after the Dewey Decimal system of classification used in libraries.

At the first meeting, vote one member to be the archivist. He is responsible for keeping a journal about the SSBR's activities. This will include a list of the books read, the members present at each meeting, and a summary of the discussion. Elect the person who is the most responsible. You do not want the secrets of your society falling into the wrong hands.

4. Triumvirates

In 60 B.C.E., 3 men joined together to rule Rome. This triumvirate was Marcus Crassus, Gnaeus Pompeius, and a fellow named Julius Caesar.

Those names may not be famous to you (the first 2, anyway), but they were a big deal then.

In their honor, compete with a friend to see who can list the most groups of 3. Whoever gets the most in 3 (obviously) minutes wins. Examples: the 3 meals of the day; the 3 branches of government in the United States; the 3 ships of Columbus; the 3 blind mice; the 3 Musketeers; the 3 Stooges; the 3 Rice Krispies elves; the 3 occupations mentioned in "Rub-a-Dub-Dub"; and the 3 inalienable rights specified in the Declaration of Independence (life, liberty, pursuit of happiness). And there are many more.

5. Write a Character's Back Story

Everyone you pass on the street has a life story.

Same with every character in a book, even if he appears for only one scene. That story may be much more interesting than you'd guess!

Pick a minor character from a book whose back story (events that happened to him before the story began) is not given. Make one up for him, using any details the book does give about him to guide you. (If the book doesn't give any information about that character, you have a lot more flexibility!)

- Where was he born?

- What was his early childhood like?

- What were his dreams?

- How did he meet the characters in the book?

You might find that this minor character is interesting enough to star in a book of his own.

6. Play Forbidden Letters

If you're a voracious reader, this game should be as easy for you as reciting the alphabet.

1. Make a list of 10 categories—foods, animals, colors, rock stars, candy bars, and so on. Just be sure that each category has a lot of possibilities—for example, don't use "planets in our solar system" because there are only 9.

2. Ask a sibling or friend to do the same, but don't look at each other's lists.

3. One at a time, ask each other to quickly name one example that fits each of your categories—but there's a catch. For each game, one letter is forbidden, and no answer can contain that letter. For example: if "a" is forbidden and the category is "countries," "Egypt" works but "Italy" would disqualify you.

4. Once you each go through all of your categories, play again with different forbidden letters, or even think of 10 new categories.

7. Save Yourself

When you think of saving in the summertime, you might think of lifeguards rescuing imperiled swimmers from a choppy sea (or maybe a swimming pool).

But there's another important type of saving—saving money. Either alone or with partners, set up a neighborhood money-making endeavor that will last 3 days, such as drawing cartoon portraits, building Web sites, doing yard cleanup, or planting vegetables.

Set aside ⅓ of your earnings at the end of the first day, ⅓ on the second day, and ½ on the final day. Use that money to open (or contribute to an existing) savings account. That doesn't mean you need to spend the remaining money—by all means save some of that, too, if you can. It's good practice for when you're older, when you'll need to save at least ⅓ of your income for taxes, college tuition for your own kids, retirement, and more.

But back to the present: do buy yourself a little something now with your earnings. You worked too hard not to.

8. Food Web Puzzle

In nature, every living thing has an appetite.

Luckily, most of them live where they can satisfy it—until they satisfy something else's appetite. It's weird to realize that the main reason some animals are here is to be some other animal's main source of food. Find and print or copy an example of a food web (sometimes called a food chain).

Make a card for each living thing. Without looking at the original, try to re-create the food web with the cards. Then challenge siblings and friends to do the same.

For example:

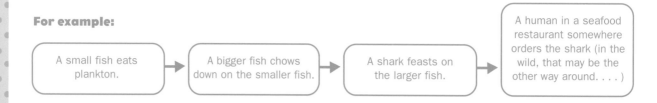

A small fish eats plankton. → A bigger fish chows down on the smaller fish. → A shark feasts on the larger fish. → A human in a seafood restaurant somewhere orders the shark (in the wild, that may be the other way around. . . .)

9. Book Bookmarks

Don't dog-ear your books—make bookmarks to use instead.

Here's a fun way to revisit your favorite reads. Make bookmarks that feature capsule summaries of the books you liked best during the past year. If you don't have access to a computer, cut thin cardboard into standard bookmark-sized strips that you can write on. If you do have a computer, create a bookmark-sized template, type your summary onto it, and print it out. Use any graphic design elements you want as long as you leave room for the text. The challenge is to describe all the key characters and elements of the book in that short space. It's almost like a preview for the book.

10. Objects from Where?

Pick an item you own, such as a book or a baseball bat, and trace it back to where it came from. No, not the mall—all the way to the Earth.

Paper and wooden bats are both made from wood, which comes from forests. But what kind of wood, and from what part of the world? What about the hard covers of some books?

What about aluminum bats? Where does the aluminum come from—in which countries is aluminum mined? How is it changed from the form in which it's found in the ground (usually bauxite) to the metal we recognize as aluminum?

Do some detective work for your item, which may require you to call the company that manufactures your item to inquire about its materials' origins. Even the simplest objects may turn out to be built from parts from around the world.

11. Measure Melting

Introducing a new measurement to rival mph (miles per hour): mtm (minutes to melt).

1. Fill two identical plastic cups, one with water and the other with milk. Both should contain the same level of liquid.

2. Put both in the freezer.

3. When they're frozen solid, remove them and time how long it takes each to melt completely. To do this, pour the melted portion of each into separate empty cups every 10 minutes and observe which is melting faster.

4. Repeat the experiment with any other drinkable liquids like apple juice versus orange juice or liquidy solids like pudding versus butter. You can even try 2 versions of the same drink, such as pulp-free OJ and pulp-crazy OJ.

5. Try to come to a conclusion about the rate at which something melts. Does it seem like a substance's consistency affects its mtm?

12. Contribute to (or Create) a Blog

Blogs are online journals that can be read by anyone with access to a computer.

People write whatever they're doing and feeling, sometimes on a daily basis, and post it on the Internet. Search "blog" and skim a few to get the idea.

Find a blog specifically about an interest of yours and see if kids can post to it. At all times, ask a parent to supervise where you surf and what you post. If you're tech-savvy, perhaps you can create your own blog—or perhaps you have already. Can you think of a way to create a blog without using the Internet? Maybe a handwritten blog on a huge sheet of paper on your bedroom wall, on which anyone who visits can "post" by writing a response to the last comment?

13. Start Spreading the News

It took Christianity 300 years to become generally accepted throughout the Roman empire. That may seem slow to you, but by history's standards, it was quite fast.

See how fast *you* can spread an idea. That idea will simply be a quotation that you like—it can be funny or serious, silly or smart.

Rewrite the following note on a sheet of paper, filling in the blanks as you go (but don't rewrite the directions in parentheses—those are just to help you!).

This is one of my favorite quotations: _____ (write one of your favorite quotations or song lyrics). *My name is* _____. *I am trying an experiment from the book* Summer Activities. *I want to see how many people will duplicate and pass along my quotation in one week. Please rewrite this entire note on another sheet of paper. Then pass the notes to different people and ask them both to do the same. If you receive this note on* _____ (fill in the date one week after you hand out your original note), *please mail it to me at* _____ (provide your mailing address). *That way, I will learn how far the experiment spread and how many people read my quotation. Thank you!*

14. Heat Transfer Toss

There are 3 forms of heat transfer, and they sometimes overlap.

Convection involves the transfer of heat within a fluid, such as a liquid or a gas like the air around us. Examples: warm water rises in a lake while cold water descends; you feel the heat of a wood stove when you stand next to it (which is also a characteristic of radiation) as heat in the room moves with the warm currents from warmer areas to cooler areas.

Conduction involves the transfer of heat from something solid to something else solid, which requires direct contact. Examples: a thermometer under your tongue shows a high fever; a spoon in cocoa gets hot.

Radiation involves the transfer of heat through empty space. Examples: the sun sends its heat to Earth through space; on cloudless nights heat escapes from Earth and goes into the atmosphere.

Label a series of same-sized pails or other containers marked with these 3 forms. Make a series of examples of each and write them on index cards. Ask friends to toss each card into the correct bucket, something that takes both knowledge *and* aim!

15. Match Beginnings with Endings

This is not a test of your knowledge. It's a test of your memory.

Okay, so maybe that's related to knowledge. Anyway, check books out of the library that you read during the school year. It should be no fewer than 5 books, and the ideal number is 10 (or more!). Get a pack of index cards. Write the first sentence from each book on its own card, and then the last sentence of each book on its own card. Call a meeting of friends from your class to play a game. Shuffle all the cards, then lay them on the ground in a grid, like the card game Concentration (also known as Memory)—only here place all the cards face up. One at a time, everyone tries to match the first and last sentence from the same book, which the others must verify. For extra credit, name the book both sentences are from.

16. License Plate Addition

Make a list of 10 significant numbers in your life, such as your age, the day of the month you were born, your house or apartment number, and your lucky number if you have one.

Bring the list on your next family car trip—even if it's just to the movies. Compete with a sibling or friend who also made a list—and is also in the car—to see who can be the first to check off his whole list. How? By adding numbers in passing license plates. For example, if your birth date is the seventh, you need to find a license plate with numbers that add up to 7 (ignore any letters in each license plate). So if the license plate is:

then you can cross that one off your list because $5 + 0 + 1 + 1 = 7$.

All players should decide in advance whether parked cars count. Also, since this is a fast-moving game, trust is important. You may not see a certain plate that your competitor uses, but you should take his word for it—or find a more trustworthy competitor!

17. Heat Is Relative

Any place on Earth where there are living things, there is heat.

However, heat is relative. Even though it can get very cold in Siberia, there is enough heat there for certain animals to live. And even though a northern winter night is frigid, it's not nearly as cold as a northern winter night on, say, Pluto, which is much farther from the warmth of the sun.

Make a mini-book about the degrees of heat on Earth to show that our planet is always heated. Start it with, "An Antarctic night in winter is hot, but not compared to . . . ," then turn the page and write something just a little warmer, such as ". . . an Antarctic day in winter." Do some research, choose examples that get gradually warmer (which will also be getting closer to the equator), and illustrate the book.

18. Caption Your Family Album

Family photo albums can bore people till they drool.

Make it your mission to liven up one of yours. Find an album that has no captions. As you go through it, think of captions for the photos, write them on sticky notes and post them alongside the photos. Then look through the album again with your family. Hopefully they'll laugh at themselves as much as you did!

Here are some examples to charge up your creativity. If you use them, this book can't be held responsible for any complaints. However, it will happily accept any compliments.

For a photo of:

- **You as a baby:** "Me at the 'Cutest Baby in the World' photo shoot."

- **Your sibling as a baby:** "[Insert sibling name] right after mom and dad picked him up at the zoo."

- **Your dad in an ugly tie:** "Yes, it's an ugly tie, but no, it wasn't a Father's Day gift."

- **Your mom pregnant with you:** "I probably shouldn't have eaten that 4th pizza."

19. When You're 33

In 12 years, Alexander the Great expanded the Greek empire to include almost all of the lands the Greeks knew about at the time.

Alexander was not an old general—he died at age 33. Though world domination is probably not in your plans, you might have an idea of what you'd like to be when you grow up.

Write a prediction about what you'll be doing when you're 33, then seal it in an envelope and write on the envelope "Do Not Open till I'm 33 Years Old."

Put it with your most cherished possession, one you know you'll have your whole life, so you don't risk losing the envelope. Then relax for a little more than 2 decades until the big moment arrives when you can open this prediction. Maybe you'll even still have this book, too.

20. Read Where It Happened

Books are supposed to take you to a place you haven't been before. Now try taking a book to place it _has_ been.

Find a book whose setting is near where you live or someplace you are visiting. For example, if you live in or are visiting New York City, read _The Cricket in Times Square_, by George Selden, there.

Close enough is good enough. If the book you want to read takes place in one town in, say, Idaho, and you live in another town in Idaho, no worries—that counts. It also doesn't have to be a specific place, which is helpful if you live in the middle of nowhere. If the book takes place at or has a key scene at the beach, head to _any_ nearby beach with the book to read—even if the beach in the book is named but is nowhere near you. While the author probably didn't write the book specifically to be read in certain settings, it may enhance your reading experience to immerse yourself more completely in the locations described in the book.

21. Stuff Your Face Race

Here's a way to eat and exercise at the same time.

1. Set up 2 tables with an identical selection of a variety of small, healthy foods such as blueberries, thin apple slices, and cashews. Be precise—if table 1 has 18 blueberries, table 2 must have exactly 18 also.

2. Nominate someone to be the game master. She might want to make a list of her commands in advance so she doesn't have to think on her feet like the players do!

3. Two teams line up about 25 feet (7.62 m) away, parallel, each team facing one of the tables.

4. When the game master calls out, "Go!" the first member of each team races to the table and eats whatever the game master commands—and that command will be in terms of fractions. For example, "Eat ⅔ of the raisins." So if there are 6 raisins, each player must eat 4 of them.

5. Run back and tag the next player, who runs to the table and does the same ("Eat ⅙ of the crackers").

6. Whichever team has completed more eating tasks correctly wins, even if that team is slower. The game master must keep track. This can be played with as few as 2 (hungry) people.

22. Follow the String Silk Road

The Silk Road was an ancient trade route between China and the Roman Empire.

It wasn't a single road, nor was it made of silk, but silk was one of the key commodities transported along various routes.

Create 2 matching versions of the Silk Road and set up a race between 2 explorers (in other words, friends) to see who knows more about what was traded along the original. Cut 2 looooong pieces of string, each about 500 feet (150 m) long—make sure they're exactly the same length.

Get a total of 20 index cards and divide them into 2 piles of 10. On each card in the first pile, write the

name of a different good that was or was not traded along the Silk Road. That's one good per card.

Things that were traded:

- Jades
- Bronzes
- Peacocks
- Gunpowder
- Ceramic crafts
- Fur
- And more (check books and online to add to this list)

Things that weren't traded:

- Milk
- Eyeglasses
- Eyelashes
- Pencils
- Matches
- Cannonballs
- And much, much more

Rewrite the same selection of goods on the second pile of 10 cards.

Attach the 10 cards from the first pile in random order along the first string, then repeat with the second pile of cards and the second string. Snake both strings somewhat parallel but in a crazy pattern through a safe outdoor area, such as a back-yard. Run them under, over, around, and through things like jungle gyms or lawn furniture. Then send a friend along each route, racing to pick up only the goods that were actually traded along the original Silk Road. Whoever gets more right wins, regardless of who gets to the end first.

23. Build a _____ Castle

In a weird way, books and beaches go together.

Both have tons of tiny dots—in books they're periods, while at the beach, they're grains of sand.

Bring a dictionary to the beach—which might be a world's first! Form teams of you and your friends, even if only one person is on each team. To play the game, a member of each team opens the dictionary and points to somewhere on the page without looking. When each pointer's finger has landed on top of a noun, her team has to try to build whatever it is out of sand—and it almost certainly won't be a castle! If your noun is impossible to build, try drawing it in the sand, and if even that is too difficult, randomly pick a different noun. Don't tell the other team or teams what your noun is.

When everyone is done building, each team must guess what the other team or teams built.

24. Create a Current

The Gulf Stream is something like a fast-moving river within the Atlantic Ocean.

A few hundred years ago, the Gulf Stream helped propel ships from the New World back to Europe much faster than many explorers expected. It still does, plus it warms the climates of the regions it passes.

With adult supervision, place the end of a hose into the water of a pool, just below the surface. Keep the hose parallel to the surface of the water and turn it on. The "river" within the pool water is a simple version of a current like the Gulf Stream. Put a toy boat in the pool and see how fast it floats to the other side of the pool, then compare it to the path and speed of the boat when it's in the current you created.

25. Beat the Heat (and Your Friends)

You're not one of those people who always switches on the air-conditioning to cool off, are you? A bit lazy, don't you think? Forget convenience—time for genius.

Compete individually or in teams to invent a portable personal cooling device. Defrost your mind to frost your body—low temps can be low tech. Examples include a stop-the-sweat scarf (ice cubes placed in a large plastic bag) or a hat with an oversized brim for shade and a battery-operated, clip-on fan. Your parents or siblings can be the judges. The winner is whoever made the device that is so effective that its demonstrator is the last to reach for the air-conditioner switch.

26. Make Your Case—In Writing

The pen can be mightier than the tongue.

Is there something you want—and feel it's fair for you to want it—but your parents have said no every time you've asked? Rather than just complain or demand, try a different approach and you might win them over. Write a persuasive note to explain clearly and sensibly why you want what you want. Even if you've already said it, putting it on paper helps you choose your words and your points even more carefully, allowing you to make a stronger case. No word limit— use just enough to change minds.

Here are some tips on persuasion. Hopefully, you will be persuaded to try some of them:

- Be passionate but not defensive. Using an angry or whiny tone might even get on your own nerves!

- Put yourself in your parents' position. If you understand why they're saying no, you might see a new way to approach the situation.

- If you have more than one reason, order them most important to least important. But include only real reasons. Persuasion is not deception!

- Keep it short. Even shorter than this entry, if you can.

27. Stage a Debate

Here's an activity you _will_ argue with.

Choose 2 countries or cultures that you learned about this past school year—countries that fought a war with each other or that disagreed on some issue, such as boundaries, politics, or religion. It can be a pair from any era you have studied in school. You will represent one of the cultures, and a sibling or friend will stand in for the other. After you both familiarize yourself with the facts, have a public debate in which you each explain your points of view to an audience (other family members and friends). Perhaps you'll be able to come to a peaceful solution better than our ancestors did. For maximum authenticity, dress in period clothing.

28. The Pi of Pie

No matter how big or small, every circle has something in common.

When a circle's circumference (the length of the outside of the circle) is divided by its diameter (the length of a line that goes through the center of the circle), the answer will always be 3.14. Actually, it will be 3.1415926 . . . and so on for literally millions of digits. So let's stick with 3.14. This mathematical magic is called pi, often written symbolically as π.

Test out the pi theory on a more delicious pie—be it cherry, apple, blueberry, ice cream, or even turkey pot. Use a string to measure the circumference of the pie. Do this by wrapping it around the edge of the pie until it meets the point you started from, marking that point, and placing the string against a ruler to get the length. Use the ruler to measure across the center of the pie to find the diameter. Divide the second number into the first. Pi? Aye. Then do the same thing on a different-sized—but still round—pie.

To celebrate a successful experiment, dig in—but don't eat both pies in one sitting. Trust me, you'll regret it.

29. Make a Prayer Wheel

Take this activity for a spin.

Buddhism reached Tibet in the late 7th century C.E. Tibetan religious men called monks use devices called prayer wheels to say prayers. Each rotation of the prayer wheel is the equivalent of reading or reciting the sacred text enclosed inside the cylinder of the wheel one time.

The appearance and size of prayer wheels can vary (some are made of metal, some of wood, and they can be hand-held or several yards in diameter and turned by the wind or flowing water), but they are usually mounted on a handle and they are always spun clockwise.

Make your own prayer wheel. Do an online image search for "prayer wheel" to see what it should look like, but don't feel limited—or intimidated—by what you find. Yours can take any form you're comfortable with, as long as it is something that can turn round and round.

Here's one simple way to make one. Decorate a piece of 8½-by-11-inch (22.6-by-27.9 cm) paper any way you'd like. Loop it around and tape one of the 8½-inch (22.6 cm) ends to the other. You already have your cylinder!

Place the cylinder upright on another piece of paper and trace the circular base. Cut that circle out and poke one small hole in its center with a pin. Tape the circle to one end of the cylinder and stick a sharpened pencil partially into the small hole inside the cylinder to make a prayer wheel that spins. (Don't push the pencil in too much or it will slide right into the cylinder—and you'll lose your handle!)

Finally, attach your own prayers to your prayer wheel on small sticky notes, and if you want, ask your family and friends to do the same. Spin it and see what happens.

30. Compare Two Types of Plays

Summer is the time to come out and "play."

Check 2 books out of the library—a stage play (meaning a traditional play, one performed in a theater) and a screenplay (to be performed in a film). They don't have to be of the same story.

Compare both formats. Are there any features one form has but the other does not? Do you enjoy reading stories in these formats? Why or why not? Do you think they can be appreciated on their own, or do you think they need to be performed or filmed to be complete?

If you've still got energy, find a novel version of either the stage play or the screenplay and compare that to the play version. Which do you like better?

31. Write Your Autobiography

Don't wait for some high-profile celebrity journalist to nab the rights to your life story—write it yourself first.

Jot down a brief outline of the key events in your life, year by year. You may have had situations that are major but perhaps too personal to include. You can either try writing about them and see if it feels comfortable or you can leave those parts for the sequel, when you'll be older and perhaps willing to reveal more about yourself. The autobiography can be as short or as long as you want. The goal is not simply to get all your favorite events into the story but to describe them with flair—your life may be unbearably exciting, but your writing must be too or no one will want to read it.

Share your work with family and friends if you'd like, or keep it to yourself. It's your life.

The service can be great. The décor can be wonderful. The location can be convenient. But if the food isn't good, a restaurant isn't worth it.

With a sibling or friend, size up the popularity of 2 nearby restaurants (your favorite and his favorite) by taking a tally of cars in their parking lots at 7 P.M. (dinnertime) on a Saturday (big eating-out night). Count the total number of spaces in the lot, then the number of filled spaces. That will allow you to determine which restaurant has more cars proportionately. So, if Grilled Cheese Café has 18 spaces and 13 of those are filled, and PB&J Palace has 7 spaces and 6 are filled, what does that say? It says that GCC has 72 percent (13 ÷ 18) of its spaces filled, while PBJP has 86 percent (6 ÷ 7) filled. Even though GCC has more spaces and more cars than PBJP, it's PBJP that has a higher percentage filled.

33. Write Your Friend's Biography

You've had practice writing about someone you know everything about—yourself. Now write about someone you know *nearly* everything about—a good friend.

And what you don't know, you'll have to find out by interviewing him. As you plan how you'll write the biography, be creative—you don't have to go through his life in order. You can start with any unusual event that's happened to him, no matter how old he was at the time. That way, you'll grab readers from the start. Every biography needs a few juicy details that have not been revealed elsewhere. Just be sure your friend is okay with you being the one to go public with his story. If not, it can stay between the 2 of you.

34. Produce a News Show

History is not just about the weird outfits, strange speech patterns, and lack of indoor plumbing.

It's also what happened earlier today. Use a camcorder to report the day's events in evening news broadcast format. Use newspapers, the Internet, and even TV to learn what the local, national, and international stories of the day are, then prepare your own reports, putting your personal spin on them. Recruit siblings and friends to join your news team.

As on the 6 and 11 o'clock news, you'll need 2 lead news anchors, a meteorologist to discuss the weather, and a sports person, plus someone to man the camera. If you like being true-to-life, dress the part, too—that means jacket and tie for the boys and nice blouse or dress for the girls. You can even practice saying small jokes to one another as real newscasters sometimes do at the end of their broadcast.

You might be able to produce a segment "on the street"—meaning outside of your basement or wherever you will create your studio. One of your "reporters" and a cameraperson can go to a nearby public place such as a shopping center and get people's opinion about a local issue. Say your town is going to change the design of all the street signs.

Ask passersby what they think of that decision. If you don't have access to editing equipment, you'll have to conduct this interview segment in sequence—meaning you'll have to start your broadcast, leave to shoot this, and then come back to finish your broadcast.

Set up a news desk, hang a map behind you if you have one, review your notes, and try to do it all in one take as if you're really live.

Screen your show for family and friends.

35. Serialize a Story

In the thrilling days of yesteryear, some writers published their stories in magazines—chapter by chapter.

This stretched-out story was called a serial. Many chapters ended on a breathtaking moment, so readers would have to wait till the next issue to find out what happened. That kept readers wanting more—and therefore reading and buying more magazines. This project involves writing, but the gimmick is about the reading.

Write a dynamic short story that is broken into 5 chapters or parts. Then send a serialized e-mail version of your story to your friends—er, subscribers—one part per day for 5 days in a row (or, if you want to do it like they did in the olden days, 5 weeks in a row, one section per week).

Your challenge is to come up with 4 edge-of-your-seat moments to end each of the first 4 serialized portions with. You want your friends to wait eagerly for each installment. Maybe this will inspire one or more of them to do the same, so you'll get some exciting reading after doing all the exciting writing.

36. Division Diving

You're used to learning in a school. Have you ever learned in a swimming pool?

1. With a parent's supervision, toss at least 25 coins into a pool. Be sure to use a mixture of dimes, nickels, and lots of pennies.

2. Your parent shows you and a sibling or friend a flash card with a division problem on it.

3. You and the friend dive in (parallel, so you don't collide—and in the deep end, of course!) to retrieve whatever coins add up to the solution.

Note: You may not have the breath to get all the coins on the first dive, but that's okay. The first person to get the exact amount wins, no matter how many dives it takes. If anyone goes over the correct amount, he's out of that round. For example, if you and your friend are shown 45 ÷ 5, the first to come up with a nickel and 4 pennies—or 9 pennies—wins that round.

37. Write with the Five Senses

Sight and sound aren't the only senses: use the other 3.

Write a short story and don't limit yourself to describing sights and sounds. Write about how things smell, feel, and taste, too. This will make the story come alive even more. Combine all of the senses and use them in unexpected ways, too.

When you think "ocean," you might think of the unfathomable sight of water stretching beyond the horizon or the hypnotic sound of lapping waves. How can you bring taste into it? Nobody's drinking the ocean. But a swim in the ocean can involve the salty spray of the water into the air.

And there you have it—salty is a taste. If you look/listen/smell/touch/taste hard enough, the 5 senses really are everywhere.

38. Volunteer at a Marathon

Once upon a legend, a Persian army stormed into a Greek city near Athens called Marathon.

To seek help, a Greek soldier named Pheidippides ran from Marathon to the city of Sparta then back to Marathon, fought in the war (which the Greeks won), and ran again—approximately 26 miles (41.8 km) from Marathon to Athens, to announce the victory. Whew! The ancient Greeks invented many things, but unfortunately for Pheidippides, cell phones were not one of them.

Though some or all of this story may be fictional, it was nonetheless the inspiration for the creation of the modern 26-mile (41.8 km) footrace called the marathon. Search online to find out where and when a marathon is being held where you live (or nearby). Call the managing organization and ask if there's a way for someone your age to volunteer at the race. Perhaps you can help distribute T-shirts or hand out cups of water to runners along the route. And later, when you're old enough, maybe you'll run in a marathon yourself.

39. Read a Banned Book

Banned books are not necessarily bad books.

They're books that one person thinks someone else will be offended by. In the end, it's all personal opinion. Some American schools have banned *The Adventures of Huckleberry Finn*, by Mark Twain, accusing it of being racist. *Sylvester and the Magic Pebble*, by William Steig, has been banned for portraying police officers as pigs. Even *Where's Waldo?* has been banned.

But books are written to be read, not hidden. Books written to be hidden are called diaries. Can't they keep it straight?

Find a list of books that at least one U.S. school has banned sometime in the last 10 years—and hopefully your school wasn't one of them. Then read every book on it. Get a friend to do the same. Discuss. Do you think any of those books should have been banned? Why do you think they were banned? How did they affect you?

Here are a few more books that have been banned:

- *The Chocolate War* by Robert Cormier
- The Harry Potter series by J.K. Rowling
- *In the Night Kitchen* by Maurice Sendak
- *The Goats* by Brock Cole
- *Blubber* by Judy Blume

Afterward, you'll probably ask yourself this question: if people are going to go around banning books, why does it have to be the most interesting ones? Then you might ask this: if they cannot resist the urge to censor something, why don't they just let up on all the rest and ban the phone book instead? It's so long and boring, plus it's all online now anyway.

40. Stage a Gold Rush

Throughout history, few things have gotten people moving quicker than the discovery of gold.

Collect an assortment of rocks and turn them into gold using nontoxic paint that an adult has bought with you. Gather a crew of bold gold hunters and set your sights on your backyard. By random drawing, determine which of you will hide the gold while the others hide their eyes—or better yet, go inside until all rocks are out of sight. (First count the rocks so you'll know when to stop looking!) Then set out on a gold scavenger hunt.

When all the nuggets are found, tally up the worth of each by whatever system you devise. Say big stones are worth $100, medium-sized stones are worth $50, and small stones $25. Whoever finds the most "gold" wins. Actually, the real winner would be anyone who happens to find any *real* gold. . . .

41. Recycle without Leaving Home

Save yourself a trip to the curb.

Think about the ways you can recycle things in your own house. That empty plastic peanut butter jar—clean it and use it to store those extra buttons that come with new shirts and that always seem to get lost. Keep newspapers so you can use them as drop cloths when you paint your masterpieces or for your parents to use as packing material when they send you care packages at camp.

Or channel your inner inventor and get totally wild. Is there a way you can rig some clean tin cans and string to be an alarm for your room—one that automatically drops to scare off intruders (a.k.a. nosy brothers or sisters)? Can you cut an empty gallon milk jug in a certain way to make it a remote control container?

Revisit your recyclables before rejecting them. They may come in handy yet again.

Free double-scoop ice cream cones for all!

Did that get your attention? Just like books, articles in newspapers and magazines need an attention-grabbing opening line to get readers to keep reading.

Go get one issue of your favorite magazine. Then, compare the first sentence of every article. Do the same with every article of a weekly news magazine such as *Time* or *Newsweek*. Keep a tally answering the following questions:

1. How many articles start with a line that entices you to read further? (This is about the first sentence only—not one sentence more.)

2. How many articles begin with a brief story about a person rather than a straight explanatory opening?

3. Do you prefer one of those 2 styles over the other?

If you find an opener that bores you to babbling, read the rest of the article anyway, then try rewriting that first line.

43. Make a Complimentary Cake

For a friend's birthday, don't just put candles on the cake. Tell the birthday boy or girl how you really feel about them—in icing.

You'll need a squeeze tube of colored icing and a steady hand. Before you start decorating the cake, take a pencil and paper and write out a short description of your friend. Write about all her best qualities: is she smart, funny, a good all-around pal? A great soccer player or a talented artist? It's her birthday, so lay it on thick.

Once you are happy that your description will make your friend happy too, write your compliment on the cake in icing and surprise your friend. She'll enjoy the praise, and you'll enjoy eating some of your own words.

44. Hammurabi's Code

Take ancient law into your own hands.

Hammurabi's Code is one of the earliest sets of laws that clearly outlines rules and the punishments for breaking the rules. Check a world history book or online for Hammurabi's Code and its more than 200 rules for Mesopotamia from about 1790 to 1750 B.C.E. The Code was inscribed on large stone tablets and displayed for all to see. The language may seem odd in places, and some of the laws will seem painfully cruel.

Here are 3 laws, paraphrased for your reading pleasure:

- If a fire breaks out in a house and someone who comes to help put it out ends up stealing from that house, he will be thrown into that fire.

- If someone's dam is so poorly maintained that it breaks and floods the fields, the dam owner shall be sold, and the money will be used to replace the corn that has been ruined because of his laziness.

- If someone pokes out the eye of someone else, his own eye will be poked out.

Find 3 rules that could apply in America today and 3 that wouldn't. Make 2 stone tablets, one for the "would work" rules and one for the "wouldn't work" rules. Use chalk or a marker instead of a chisel to "inscribe" the 2 mini-codes.

If you can't find any stone tablets, a piece of cardboard with slightly rough edges cut into it ought to work as well.

The punishments in Hammurabi's Code are so severe that you'll wonder how anyone back then could have broken the law. Try your hand at ancient lawmaking. Choose 3 particularly harsh HC rules and come up with alternative punishments for each.

45. Throw a Tree Stump a Party

Some parents mark their kids' height at different ages up a wall.

That's harder to do with trees, since most tend to grow much taller than we do (and most aren't near walls). But you can honor a tree's age in another way.

Find a tree stump and figure out approximately how old the tree was by counting the rings on its flat top. Throw it a tree-themed birthday party—you and your friends are the guests. Make leaf-shaped cookies and ice them with green frosting. Serve a fruit salad made only of fruits that grow on trees, such as apples and peaches. Since trees can live a long time, you might need to use really small candles to fit them all on a cake. And if you want to get really nutty, make it a tree costume party—all guests must come dressed as their favorite type of tree.

46. Sit under a Tree

Despite what this book might suggest, summer does not have to be nonstop activities.

And an activity doesn't have to involve lots of friends, complex rules, and a fast pace. In about the year 528 B.C.E., a man named Siddhartha sat under a tree in Bihar, India, and was struck with ideas that would lead to the establishment of Buddhism. This religion places great emphasis on meditation, sitting quietly and paying attention to your thoughts as they come and go from your mind.

See what comes to your mind when you take a leisurely rest under a tree of your choosing. Bring a pad and pencil to jot down anything that enters your mind, whether it's brilliant or bizarre. Perhaps you have a problem you want to try to figure out, perhaps you want to come up with a creative idea of some kind, or perhaps you have no specific goal at all. In summer, it's especially nice to sit quietly under a tree, just like Siddartha did. After all, that's where all the shade hangs out!

47. Share the Wealth

Assemble a powerhouse team of siblings and friends for a good cause—and prepare for double division.

You'll be running an easy fundraiser. First, decide on how you'll make money; a few of many possible examples are a dog wash, a frozen treats sale, or even the classic lemonade stand. The first division is the division of labor. That means you'll split up tasks among the group so that everyone has an equal amount to do and everything can get done efficiently. One person can advertise the event, another can be in charge of the earnings, a third can gather any needed supplies, and so on. All of you should be present on the day of the fundraiser.

The second division comes after the event is over when your group divides the profits equally among more than one charitable organization. Every participant should choose a charity to contribute to. So, if you raise $167 and have a six-person team, you will be donating $27.83 to each charity, with 2 cents left over for good luck.

48. Give an Author a Second Chance

If you've read a book by an author you've never read before and didn't like it, don't give up on him.

Read another book by the same author (a shorter one is fine!). If part of the reason you didn't like the first book is because the subject matter didn't appeal to you, find a book about something else. You may have a completely different reaction to the second book. It may even turn out to be something you love. What if it becomes your favorite book? And you were *this close* to never discovering it. After all, if you see a movie with a star you like but don't like the movie, you'll still see another movie with that same star, right?

Try variations on this experiment requiring 2 books by the same author. Say you read 2 books by one author—you hated the first but liked the second. Give that author a tiebreaking third chance. If you like the third book, the first may be a fluke.

Another variation involves an author's writing style. Choose any 2 books by an author. They must be ones you're unfamiliar with. Read both, then guess which book the author wrote first. Maybe these 2 books are separated by a year, maybe 20. Do you see any differences in the author's writing style? Did you sense one was written better than the other—and was that the newer book?

49. From Fable to Theater

Aesop's fables are real, of course, but Aesop himself wasn't.

Evidence suggests that all those famous tales—including "The Boy Who Cried Wolf" and "The Tortoise and the Hare"—were not written by a single author. More likely, a number of people compiled them over an unknown period of years in ancient Greece, but somehow it was "Aesop" who got all the credit.

Produce a mini-play based on one or more of Aesop's fables. Since fables feature animals, you'll need actors who can transform into convincing beasts and costumes to match. When done, ask all in your audience to write down what they think the moral (or lesson) of the fable is—but anonymously. Then mix up the responses and read them aloud to see how similar they are. That may be as entertaining as your play!

50. Attend a Book Signing

Authors are real people out there in the real world.

That might have been an author behind you and your mom in line at the supermarket. Or maybe it was the woman in front of you. (Probably not both, though.)

No need to guess who the authors are—there's an easy way to go meet one. Check the calendar or newsletter of your local bookstore to see when an author you like will be appearing. Authors often make bookstore appearances to promote their latest book and meet their fans. It's typically called a book signing, for a reason that must be obvious! You might think the honor is all yours, but most authors are also honored when readers come to meet them: they're not writing books only for themselves. It could be crowded, but have at least one question in mind to ask the author. You might have a chance to ask it.

51. Find Water with a Dowsing Rod

The Earth is not hollow.

It's also not transparent, though some people claim that they can "see" what's under the surface by a process called *dowsing* using a device called a dowsing rod.

Throughout history, the dowsing rod generated a lot of controversy for such a simple instrument. As with many unexplained things, people thought dowsing was phony or even evil. Today, some people use 2 pieces of bent wire that allegedly cross when they walk over underground water. Others use a forked stick that allegedly turns in the direction of under-

ground water. One theory states that a dowsing rod moves because it's responding to the human body's sensitivity to magnetism or some other unknown force. Yet no one has proven that dowsing really works. Still, it's fun and easy to try.

Hold a forked stick or a piece of wire bent into an L-shape and walk outside over natural terrain. If your instrument moves, call your town's conservation department to ask if there is any known underground water in that area, such as a natural well or spring.

52. How Long Are Your Songs?

Everyone has his own soundtrack for the summer.

Look at your favorite CD and figure out its mean and its range based on the length of each song. The *mean* is the average length of the album's songs, and the *range* is the difference between the longest and the shortest songs' lengths.

While you're at it, figure out the *median* of the song times. To do this, rewrite all the song times in order from shortest to longest. If there is an odd number of songs, the median is the one in the middle.

For example, if the songs on a 5-song CD are:

1:58, 2:56, 3:31, 3:37, 4:10
The median song length is **3:31**

If there is an even number of songs, add the 2 middle ones together and divide by 2:

2:56, 3:31, 3:37, 4:10
The median is **3:34**
(3:31 + 3:37 ÷ 2)

And is there a mode? Are any 2 songs the same length? The *mode* is the length of a song that occurs most frequently.

53. Peloponnesian Rematch!

From 431 to 404 B.C.E., Sparta and Athens, considered the 2 most important of the ancient Greek city-states, fought.

The battle became known as the Great Peloponnesian War, and Sparta eventually won.

You can have a rematch without armor and bloodshed and in a much shorter period than the original. All you need is a checkerboard, some plastic army soldiers, paint and a thin paintbrush, and a colorful imagination.

Refer to pictures of Athenian and Spartan soldiers and paint half of your army soldiers to look Athenian and the other half Spartan. Set up the checkerboard and place a soldier on each space a checker typically goes. Then play checkers normally—and maybe, thousands of years later, Athens might finally get a victory.

54. Slimming Down Summaries

You're about to transform a book from thousands of words into about 20—or even fewer.

After reading a book that you like, write a one-page summary of it. You may think you have to leave out a lot of good stuff, but that's the idea. You're practicing the valuable art of condensing—part of knowing what to write is knowing what to leave out. But you're not done.

Then write a one-*paragraph* summary of the same book. (And no, your paragraph can't be a page long.) Finally, write a one-*line* summary of the book. For

ideas on those, check the copyright pages of young-adult novels. Many have just such a summary.

There's a saying, "Less is more." Do you think that's true?

55. Read the Rest of Something

You know the words to "The Star-Spangled Banner" (or at least some of them).

You actually know less than you think—the song has 3 more verses beyond what is commonly sung. Look them up and read them (no singing required). Find other examples of songs and poems that we're not getting the full story on and read what you've been missing.

Another example is the Henry Wadsworth Longfellow poem "Paul Revere's Ride"—it's the one that begins, "Listen, my children, and you shall hear / Of the midnight ride of Paul Revere." There's more to it than those famous opening lines. If you need help thinking of more songs or poems, ask a librarian.

56. Today's Hieroglyphs

In the modern world, trends can come and go in a matter of weeks.

In ancient Egypt, the style of art and fashion did not change much in 3,000 years! It seems they knew a cool thing when they saw it.

The ancient Egyptians used a hieroglyphic alphabet, that is, one using pictorial symbols instead of letters as we know them. Make your own ancient Egyptian-style art by drawing several people of today, real or imagined, in Egyptian style. This means you'll have the somewhat stiff bodies and side-view heads that instantly identify Egyptian art, but also possibly nose rings, baggy jeans, cell phones, MP3 players, and other common sights in the modern world. Then make up your own hieroglyphic symbols to go with the art.

57. Build a Lean-to at Sixty

You sleep on top of a sheet, but you can also sleep *under* one—by using a sheet to make your very own lean-to.

A lean-to is a makeshift shelter consisting of a short, tilted wall, usually made of wood, and two vertical sticks to hold it up. The tops of both vertical sticks are attached to the top 2 corners of the wall and the bottoms are stuck in the ground. Lean-tos can also have side walls of wood.

Create a simple lean-to—but yours won't be made of wood, and it won't have side walls. You just need a sheet and two tall, sturdy sticks or poles of some kind. Set up the lean-to at a 60° angle, which will make it a giant 30°-60°-90° triangle. You see, all triangles have 3 interior angles, and the 30°-60°-90°

kind of triangle has one angle at 30°, one at 60°, and one at 90°. In your lean-to, the 60° angle will be the one in which you'd sleep.

A protractor is probably too small to guide you here, but there's another easy way to get that angle. Using your heel, draw a line on the ground where the bottom edge of your lean-to will be. It should be a little longer than the length of your body when you're lying down. Next, measure the length of your sheet to find out how wide the tilted wall of your lean-to will be—let's say it's 5 feet (1.5 m) wide. (In other words, the "wall" itself would be 5 feet (1.5 m) tall if it were standing upright.)

To figure out how far out to place the 2 poles that will hold up your lean-to, divide the width of the wall by 2. In this case, that equals 2½ feet (0.75 m). So mark another line on the ground 2½ feet (0.75 m) out from the lean-to base. It should be parallel to and the same length as the first line you made.

Attach the sheet to the tops of the poles with tape or elastic bands. Finally, stick the poles into the ground on either end of that second line and use rocks to secure the sheet at the base. This completes the triangle—uh, lean-to. And the angle you've created will be 60°!

When the lean-to is done, lie under it and gaze out at the night sky. Perhaps you'll see a shooting star streak down, perhaps at a 60° angle. . . .

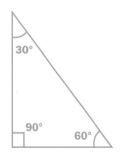

58. Dress like a Phoenician

Everyone has walked like an Egyptian. Try dressing like a Phoenician.

Among the early Mediterranean traders were the sea-faring Phoenicians, who dyed much of their clothing purple and therefore became known as the Purple People.

Pick some clothing that you can dye purple—with parental approval and supervision, of course. Create a purple pattern, the likes of which has not been seen since ancient times. Supplement your dyed clothes with any existing purple clothes you may own.

You can take this a step further and host a purple-themed feast, featuring only purple foods—grapes, eggplant, plums, radicchio, and any others you can think of.

59. Compare New and Old Books

What a difference a decade can make.

Go to the library and visit the autobiography section. Find 2 books on the same person—one that has the oldest publication date and one that has the most recent. It can be on any person you're interested in, from Joan of Arc to Jackie Robinson. (Ideally the books will be at least 30 years apart—if not, keep looking until you find 2 books that are.)

Read the first chapter of each book. Is one more exciting than the other? Does one seem more like a textbook than the other? Does one read more like a story than the other? Then do a blind read to a sibling or friend, reading the first page of each book aloud and making sure he can't see the cover. Ask which book sounds more "modern."

60. Relay Story

Have you ever run a relay race? You and some friends are going to write a relay story.

A relay race is one that has multiple runners, each running a smaller segment of the whole race. One runner starts the race holding a baton, which he passes to the next runner at the start of the next portion of the race, and so on. You are going to do the same thing with your story. One person will start the story off by writing one page. He will then hand it to another friend, who will continue the story, also writing a page. If a group of 5 friends is participating, the finished story will have 5 pages. You don't all have to be there at the same time to do this—it may take a week or longer for everyone to contribute their portions.

The goal you all must keep in mind is to keep the story coherent, sticking with some key elements already established while adding some of your own. In other words, if the first page is about a cowboy who changes careers to become a ninja, and you're next in line, don't kill the cowboy-ninja off on the top of your page and start telling a story about a shark that can talk to humans. You might as well be writing separate stories to begin with if that's your attitude! The point here is to rise to the challenge of continuing someone else's story while making it your own, too.

That is not to say you shouldn't make it too easy for the writers who will come after you. Create a tricky situation that they must work their way out of—in time to end with their own tricky situation.

If your gang can't get together at the same time, do this by e-mail. It's easy to forward and can build fast.

If some of your friends aren't writers, get them involved anyway. Instead of asking everyone to contribute a page, ask for just one paragraph per person. This approach also works well if you have lots of participants. That way, you won't end up with a story that runs on too long.

When done, read your story aloud to family and friends. It's sure to get a laugh a page and probably more.

61. Review a Review

Everything gets reviewed—movies, books, restaurants, cars, software, and much more.

A reviewer's job is to explain why he did or didn't like something, so he should be cool when his own work is reviewed.

Read a review of a book you've read, then write a review of the review. Is *it* well written? Does it do a good job evaluating the book? You may think so even if you don't agree with the opinion of the reviewer.

Lastly, do you think the review overlooks or even misunderstands any key points?

You can find book reviews in magazines and newspapers, and many bookselling Web sites post reviews for each book. Just remember that there's always a way to say you didn't like something without being mean about it.

You don't have to be a giant to draw like one.

Draw a picture of anything you want. Use a ruler to pencil a grid over it in which each square is one inch by one inch. When done, it will look like your drawing has been printed on graph paper.

Then create a larger version of the grid on a huge piece of paper or on a blacktop with chalk. Again, each square will be the same size, but they will be larger than the first grid (say, one foot by one foot). Use the gridlines to reproduce your original drawing so it becomes enormous. In other words, rather than enlarging your entire picture at once, enlarge it box by box—a less overwhelming task.

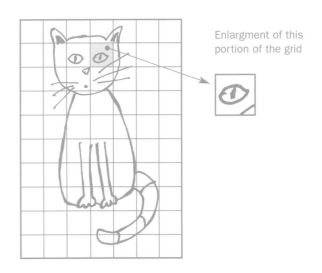

Enlargment of this portion of the grid

63. Film a Reenactment

Most of history wasn't caught on tape.

Announce a casting call to your family and friends for a new movie you'll be filming about a historical event you learned about in social studies. Of course, this means you'll first need to determine your cast of characters. Once you've got your talent, round up any required costumes and props and scout locations for your filming. Stick with approved private property—such as your yard or a friend's—since you'll need official permission from the town or city government to shoot on certain types of public property.

Use a camcorder to make your film, and keep it short. That will give you an incentive to make sure it's exciting from the start. Also, film it in the order you want the scenes to appear, unless you have access to editing equipment. Then have a world premiere night in your family room. You can even serve snacks that tie into the era of your film. For example, if your film is about ancient Rome, poke around the library to find what types of food the Romans ate.

64. Active and Dormant

Volcanoes come in many varieties, but one of the most important distinctions is whether they're active (likely to erupt) or dormant (seemingly unlikely to erupt).

1. Get a sibling or friend to play a game in which you both try to surround yourselves with only "safe," dormant volcanoes.

2. Using books and the Web, compile a list of 10 active and 10 dormant volcanoes.

3. Get 20 index cards, hold them horizontally, fold the 2 top corners so they meet, and tape them together so that what you end up with resembles a mini-volcano.

4. Write the name and location of a different real volcano on the outside of each of the mini-volcanoes.

5. Mark the underside of each mini-volcano with an A if it's active or a D if it's dormant. Use pencil and write lightly so it doesn't show through.

6. Mix up the volcanoes in front of you. One at a time, pick a volcano you think is dormant.

7. If you're right, you keep it. If you're wrong, you must put back one of your dormant volcanoes or lose a turn.

8. At the end, whoever has collected more dormant volcanoes wins.

65. Interview and Profile

An interview is just a conversation where you plan some of your questions in advance.

Pick a person in your community and interview her. Don't ambush her on the street—call or e-mail to arrange it in advance. Tape-record the conversation so you can quote her words precisely. It can be anyone—someone you've never met but have heard about, a person who helps the community, such as a firefighter, or someone you know, like a teacher.

Avoid people you know too well, like your parents—at least for your first interview. Later you can interview your parents, too, and you may find you don't know as much about them as you thought.

Ask questions you don't know the answers to and that aren't about the person's public life (but without getting too personal, of course). For example, it'd be easy to ask a firefighter lots of questions about fighting fires, and you should, but also ask what she wanted to be when she was growing up, what she is afraid of, what does she do on her time off, or what the last good book was that she read.

After you conduct the interview, write a profile of the person. A profile is a nonfiction essay about a person written from your point of view. It includes a good amount of quotations, but also some personal interpretations you have made. Your goal is to have someone reading the profile feel like he knows her personally.

Don't forget to send your interviewee a thank-you note. Speaking of which...

66. Write a Thank-You Note

When we say "thank you," it can get lost in the conversation. But when we write it, people always notice.

Write a thank-you note to someone who may not expect it. Almost any nice gesture deserves a thank-you note in return. For example, it's courteous to write a thank-you note after someone gives you a gift or does a big favor for you like feeding your cat when you're out of town.

In person, all you'd have to say is "thank you." On paper, there's more to it. Mention the gift or kind gesture specifically. If you write in generalities ("Thanks for what you did"), your note may not seem sincere. Also, briefly explain *why* the gift or gesture meant so much to you. That will mean a lot to the person who did it.

67. Save the Sunset

Summer vacation means later bedtimes—and later sunsets. (Hopefully, the sunset comes first.)

Preserve sunsets for a month statistically—and visually. Jot down what time the sun sets each evening, then compare it with the sunset time given in the newspaper or online. Make a line graph to observe the degree of the changes. How many minutes' difference is there between the sunset on the first day of the month and the last?

Also photograph each sunset and date each photo. Even better, personalize it by having someone else take your photo with the sunset behind you as you hold a sheet of paper stating what time it is.

If you're ever up at sunrise, photograph that, too, and compare the quality of the light to that at sunset. You can even show friends a sunset photo and a sunrise photo, and ask them to guess which is which.

68. Form Two Democracies

Everyone has an opinion about everything, or so it seems.

You need a group for this one—the more people the better. Decide what you want to vote on—say, whether to watch a comedy or an action movie. Vote 2 ways: **(1) As a direct democracy.** That means everyone gets his or her own vote. **(2) As a representative democracy.** That means a small group of elected people cast votes for the whole group, like when the Senate and the House of Representatives vote on bills to become laws.

After everyone has cast their individual vote, divide your group into smaller groups by a category, such as neighborhood, age, or hair color. Maybe all the brown-haired kids form one group, all the blond kids form another, and the redheads a third. Or say your gang of friends has 8 members, representing 3 neighborhoods in your town (3 people from one, 3 people from the second, 2 people from the third). Each of those groups must elect *one* representative. Then in the second vote, only those 3 representatives vote, each on behalf of his or her neighborhood.

Is the result the same? Are more or less people watching the kind of movie they want?

69. POV Switcheroo

Even if 2 people see the same thing, they will each describe it differently.

Choose a scene from a book you like that features more than one character and that is written from one character's point of view (POV). Rewrite it from the POV of another character who is in the scene. Alternatively, do this with a short story—even one you wrote yourself. If you wrote a story about a girl who thinks her grandfather is a pirate so she follows him, rewrite the story from the grandfather's perspective. Does he realize his granddaughter is following him? If so, what does he think her reason is?

With POV, you don't know the thoughts of anyone but the POV character. So you can rewrite a story from even a minor character's perspective, but that's harder because you can only write his POV for the scenes he is in. Like in the example, you couldn't write a story from the POV of someone the grandfather works with if you also include a scene in which the grandfather is at home, since that work colleague wouldn't be there. POV Switcheroo allows you to get inside someone else's head for a change.

70. New Bases in Baseball

You have the power—the power of exponents, that is.

You're about to play baseball with all the rules you already know, except for one dramatic difference: this version has 8 bases, not 3. And they're not placed in a diamond but rather randomly spread out all over the infield. That makes home runs much, much harder!

As in baseball, you still have to run the bases in order—but to know what order to run them in, you have to know about exponents. In exponent notation, the big number is called the base (get it—*base*ball?) and the little, raised number is the exponent.

In this game, each base will have a formula written in large letters on a piece of cardboard propped upright so all can see it, and the runner must know what exponent corresponds to that formula to know what base it is.

Here are 2 examples: 3 x 3 x 3 is 3 to the third power, or 3^3, which equals 27. In this game, 3 x 3 x 3 would be third base. And 9 x 9 x 9 x 9 x 9 is 9 to the fifth power, or 9^5, which equals 59,049. In this game, 9 x 9 x 9 x 9 x 9 would be fifth base.

Did you notice that you don't need to calculate each exponent to play—you just have to recognize the meaning of each exponential equation? So write your 8 exponents on cardboard signs, scatter them around the field, and play ball!

Here's an example of how one hit would go. A batter slams one way into the outfield. He sprints to the base labeled 7—any number to the first power equals itself, so 7 is another way of writing 7^1. Then he jets to the base labeled 4 x 4, which is 4 to the second power, or 4^2. He even has time to make it to third base, which here is shown as 8 x 8 x 8, another way of writing 8^3.

Since the bases are all over the place in this version of baseball, you'll get not only a mental workout but also a physical workout, too!

71. The Delicate Ecosystem

Within an ecosystem, organisms depend on one another.

If you remove one organism from a given system, it can affect others. For example, if panda bears eat bamboo, and all the bamboos are chopped down, the panda bears will die off. It's the same if you add an organism to an ecosystem. After World War II, humans brought brown Treesnakes from somewhere else in the South Pacific to the Pacific island of Guam, which had no known brown Treesnakes, or any snakes for that matter, before. The brown Treesnakes killed off many bird species of Guam. This is an example of an invasive species—one that negatively affects its ecosystem.

Here's a way to see how complicated this inter-dependence can be. Choose an ecosystem and make a list of at least 20 organisms that live in it. You may have to do a little research first. Write each organism on its own paper cup, then build a "cup castle," which represents your ecosystem. Now try removing as many cups as you can without the castle collapsing—and you can't start from the top. You must choose from within the ecosystem.

72. Quadrilateral Workout

Get in shape—literally.

Gather a group of friends together on a large, hard outdoor surface (a blacktop playground is best). One person is the caller and shouts out various quadrilateral shapes one at a time: square, rectangle, parallelogram, rhombus, isosceles trapezoid, and kite. Everyone must then hop in that shape as fast as they can. To ensure that everyone can see the shapes, have a flat pan filled with water nearby so people can wet the soles of their shoes before their turn. If you're feeling particularly energetic, hop on one foot only.

Pump up the fun by making it a contest. To make this fair, choose 2 boundary lines that are parallel and 10 feet (3 m) apart from each other. Each shape must touch both of the boundary lines—in other words, they'll all be roughly the same size. This will prevent anyone from trying to win just by making his shape small—and therefore quick. Assign a judge to decide which shape is done the best, or the fastest, or both.

Are 4 (or 6, or 8) feet (1.2, 1.8, 2.4 m) better than 2 (0.6 m)? Find out by doing this activity in teams. That means that more than one of you must work together to create a single shape. One wrong hop and you've screwed up the shape—or crashed into each other—so this will take some strategy.

73. Get Active

Which reads better: "The boy was handed a secret note by the man in a dark coat" or "A man in a dark coat handed the boy a secret note"?

Maybe they seem similar on first read, but the first sentence is written in the **passive** voice while the second is written in the **active**—and usually better—voice. In the former, something is happening to someone, in the latter, someone is doing something actively.

Go through the first few pages of a book you like and note how often passive voice is used. Do the same with something you've written. If you have nothing handy, write that short story you've been thinking about, then go back and highlight all the passive constructions in it. See, even after you know the difference between passive and active, you still write some sentences passively—all writers do. Some passive sentences are okay, but not if active ones can do the job better.

74. Draw from a Worm's-Eye View

Few animals are as in touch with the Earth as worms are.

As earthworms burrow through soil, they mix it up, which brings air in between the particles, which helps crops grow. Think of them as finger-sized farmers.

Get a new respect for these wrigglers by seeing life from their perspective. Get down on the ground and observe some worms going about their business.

Then draw pictures of everyday things as a worm would see them, meaning from ground level looking up at something much bigger. That includes yourself. It can also include other worms encountered underground. If you don't like what you come up with, you can shred up your drawing and use it for mulch. The worms will appreciate that.

75. Past and Future Reading

Deciding what to read can seem hard. Ever wonder why?

Ask a librarian or bookstore employee how many titles the place has. You'll be amazed and might wonder how you ever decided what books to read among so many. You'll be even more amazed when you realize that's only a tiny fraction of all the books out there.

To help keep track of it all, make 2 lists. The first list will consist of books you've read recently. The second will consist of books you'd like to read. Your reading wish list can be based on recommendations from family, friends, and teachers, reviews you've read, store displays that caught your eye, and authors you like. On the list of the books you've read, rate each one on a scale of 1 to 5 (5 being the best) on the following topics: overall story, writing style, and character development. Do the same with other books as you read them and move them from your wish list to your reading log.

76. Backyard Archaeology

When you think of an archaeological dig, you might envision scientists in faraway places digging for bones and artifacts that are thousands (or even hundreds of thousands) of years old.

It's true, some archaeological digs fit that description. But archaeology isn't just about looking for stone-age tools and pottery shards. It's the study of all sorts of objects from past human lives and activities, even items from the more recent past that you find in your own backyard.

With your parents' permission, mark off a square plot of land around 4 by 4 feet (123 by 123 cm) in your backyard. Prepare a notebook where you can record your findings and zip-top plastic bags where you can store them. Then start digging and see what you turn up. A soda can, some broken glass, a tennis ball, or even an old shoe? These are all human remains that can tell you something about the inhabitants (former or current!) of your house.

Wearing gloves, transfer each of your artifacts to a separate plastic bag and number it. Then write down the number and, to the best of your ability, describe what you have found. If you don't recognize the object, write down its size, color, and shape, then show it to your friends and family to see if anyone has ideas about what its purpose might have been.

77. Pen Pal Ping-Pong

In this digital world, letter writing is slowly going away.

Most of us get e-mail every day—that thrill is gone. But we rarely get postal mail—real, handwritten letters. With no offense meant to e-mail and instant messages, go back to paper, just for a while.

Choose a friend to be your old-fashioned letter-writing pen pal during the summer—even if that friend lives next door. Vow to each write at least 3 letters over the summer, and make them chockfull of top-secret—or at least chuckle-inducing—stuff. People write things in letters they might never say in person! Three letters will cost just over a dollar in postage, so be sure to set that aside from your lucrative summer businesses.

78. Public Opinion Pet Poll

Grab a clipboard and see what the average man, woman, and child on the street thinks.

Your question: What is your favorite kind of pet? You're trying for a random sampling of the public. Since the public is a group so large you can't possibly really ask them all, a random sampling will give you a sense of the group as a whole.

Conduct not one but 2 polls—one outside a pet store during business hours and the other outside any other kind of store. Compare the answers; you want at least 30 answers in each location. Do people going in or out of the pet store have a consistent answer? If so, that's because it's a biased sampling—you're asking people who probably already like animals and pets—that's not necessarily representative of the public.

The other poll is a more accurate representation of the public, because you're not polling people in a place where the majority of people are most likely pet lovers. That's random sampling.

Don't worry if some of the results are not pro-pet—the animals won't be offended.

79. Unsentence the Scramble

Screw up some sentences for fun.

Come up with a juicy sentence about whatever comes to mind: "The boy shrieked when he saw a shark fin pop up from under the waves." It should be at least 10 words long. Write each word on a different index card. Keep a master copy of the sentence on one sheet of paper, but don't show anyone.

Scramble up the cards and challenge your friends to rebuild your sentence in the right order using the cards. Take turns doing this with each other's sentences. And keep making new sentences until your twisted is all brain—uh, your brain is all twisted.

80. Menu Mistakes

Restaurants are about good food, not good spelling.

The proof is in the menus. They're often good places to find typos, especially spelling mistakes. But you have to look closely to spot them. Maybe the daily special is listed as "Chicken Fred Steak" rather than "Chicken Fried Steak." And dessert is a slice of "Lemon Mermaid Pie" rather than "Lemon Meringue."

Next time you're in a restaurant (fast food doesn't count), first decide what you want to eat, and then go hunting . . . for mistakes. If you find any errors, don't expect a free meal for your fine eye. If the food is fantastic, you might be the only person who ever notices. Plus, your "hambugger" will taste just as delicious as a "hamburger," no matter how you spell it!

81. Make a Windmill

The graceful windmill is actually a powerful engine.

Windmills harness the natural power of the wind—which we can't use up, unlike some other resources—to perform tasks such as grinding grains or pumping water. You probably don't have piles of grain waiting to be ground or buckets of water waiting to be pumped, but no matter—you can build a simple miniature windmill for show, not service. If your construction is good and the wind cooperates, your mini-mill will spin.

A large paper or plastic cup can serve as the tower. Poke a small hole in the cup about 2 inches (5 cm) from the bottom of the cup.

To make the blades, cut 4 pieces of cardboard each about the size of a stick of gum. Tape all 4 together at one end, forming a flat plus sign (+). Poke a small hole in the center of the plus (meaning it goes through all 4 pieces of cardboard). Insert a brad (a brass fastener that has a buttonlike top attached

to 2 bendable "legs") through the hole in the cardboard pieces, then through the hole in the cup,
and spread the brad's legs apart to secure it. Pinch
each blade so it's slightly angled—make sure all
the blades are at approximately the same angle.

To weight the tower so it won't blow away, fill the cup
with small stones and close the top with masking
tape. Flip it upside down (so the small base is now
the top) and put your windmill model outside.

Wait for a breeze and see if your blades catch the
wind and rotate. If not, experiment with other
materials and shapes for the blades and try again.

82. Avoid Nothing

You might have zero interest in this activity.

The concept of "zero" as a number/numeral originates with ancient Hindus in India. If you think zero is nothing, try living without it. Keep a zero log for a day—or even an hour—and see what you couldn't do without the number 0.

Here are just a few things you couldn't do without 0:

- You might not be able to dial certain phone numbers.

- You might not be able to buy certain things.

- You couldn't say what time most TV shows begin, because they usually start on the hour or half hour, therefore requiring zeroes (8:00 P.M., 10:30 A.M. and so on).

- Actually, you couldn't watch the TV stations that have zeroes in them (channel 20, 30, and so on).

- If you want to get really technical, you couldn't use your computer, either. Computer circuitry is based on the binary system, meaning that all data is formed from ones and zeroes.

83. Capture the Solid

This variation on "Capture the Flag" is solid fun.

The sought-after object is a geometric solid, not a flag. However, you don't know which solid to expect until you get to the solid storage spot on the opposing team's side—all you know is that you are seeking either a sphere, cube, cone, cylinder, or pyramid.

Before the game starts, each team tells the other what geometric shape it'll try to capture—and from then on, all regular CTF rules apply. An added wrinkle: teams can have dummy stations with red herrings, so if one team is supposed to get a sphere, they can have a cube somewhere in the vicinity to throw the other team off—if they take the wrong solid, they lose! It's up to you what form of solids you use, such as an orange for a sphere or one of those cubic clock radios.

84. Be a Critic

A critic is someone with an opinion, even if he doesn't write for a newspaper.

A good critic is someone who can intelligently explain *why* he does or doesn't like something.

Read a book that you've heard nothing about, then write a review of it. Be specific. Also be fair—if you didn't like the book overall, was there anything that you did like about it? Similarly, if you loved a book but thought it had flaws, say so, and describe those flaws. Then compare your review with published reviews, both professional and amateur. A convenient place to find both kinds is at Amazon.com or another online bookseller. Do your views line up with anyone else's?

85. Clues to Calculate

Not all mysteries involve fingerprints and foggy nights.

Gather your family or a group of friends together to solve a different kind of mystery. To do it, you'll merely need to complete a math problem (actually two). A parent, sibling, or friend should come up with a series of math problems and write each problem on a separate piece of paper. One math problem should have a variable (such as $751 - x = 287$), while the others need to be calculated (such as $51 + 823$, $496 ÷ 8$ or 116×4).

Each person gets a math problem and then everyone walks around examining everyone else's math problem until one person figures out what x equals, then who has the problem that equals it. (In this example $x = 464$ and so the person who correctly identifies 116×4 is the winner.) You can use scrap paper to work things out.

86. Start a Good-Writing Vault

Writers get inspiration from other writers.

Sometimes it's a certain word that a writer has never used in her writing before. Other times it's just a feeling that sticks in her head after she reads something.

Start saving articles or copies of stories that you like and think are well-written. They can come from newspapers, magazines, or Web sites. You can even save articles where only one phrase stood out to you—be sure to highlight the phrase so you don't forget why you saved the clipping. Store them in a folder, envelope, or box—no need to use a real, heavy, metal vault!

As your collection grows, it will become a greater and greater resource to aid in your own writing. Any time you're stuck in your writing, open your vault to get ideas or to remind yourself how reading good writing makes you feel.

Keep in mind that you're not doing this to copy other writers but rather to expand your own writing ability.

Long before your earliest ancestors got to your region, and long before the earliest humans got there, something else probably lived there . . . something big.

Using your library and a natural history museum if there is one near you, find out what dinosaurs lived in your area. Maybe there's even a story about bones discovered in your home state. Design a sign that your town could put up to boast about its famous former residents—you know, one of those:

Also, draw a family tree that includes portraits of your relatives, and, as a joke, go back one step from your earliest known relatives—to dinosaurs.

Welcome to Mytown

(Former) Home of Diplodocus longus *and* Tyrannosaurus rex

88. Write a Guidebook to Your School

New students in a school can get lost in more ways than one.

Write a light-hearted guidebook (or pamphlet, if that seems less intimidating) about your school that you could conceivably give to a new student to help her feel more at ease. Answer the key questions every student needs to know, such as what the school rules are, where to find the restrooms, what to do if you get sick in class, whether or not students can surf the Web at school, what the dress code is, the names of the school teams, and so on.

Try to write in a lively way to put the new students at ease. And don't worry about fitting everything in—write as much or as little as you want, as long as you cover all the major concerns a new student might have.

89. Geometry Hunt

It's a no-brainer to find geometric shapes in a book (especially a geometry book, duh). See how well you can do it in the real world.

Compete with a sibling or friend to locate as many of the following geometric shapes as you can somewhere in your house or neighborhood:

- Circle
- Triangle
- Square
- Rectangle
- Parallelogram
- Trapezoid
- Rhombus
- Pentagon
- Hexagon
- Octagon

The first person to find an example of each (no copying your competitor) and photograph it wins this screwy scavenger hunt. Use digital cameras if you can since they provide a much quicker way to show what you found. And you may not count that camera as your rectangle . . . you can't use it to take a picture of itself anyway.

In the interest of fairness, all searchers are limited to the same territory, such as your block or neighborhood.

90. Was It Just Right?

Find out about the long and the short of things.

Survey 5 friends about 2 books you've all read, for school perhaps—one a short book, the other a long book. On a computer, create a 1-line questionnaire about the books and print out copies for all 5 friends. Here's the question, which should be answered for both books: "Did you find the book too long, too short, or just right?" Then leave space for them to explain their answer.

Distribute the questionnaires and give your friends a deadline. Once they've turned in their completed questionnaires, compare them. Note how many said that the long one was "too long" (that's often a sign that the person didn't like the book); note if anyone said the short book was "too short" (in most cases that's a high compliment!). Did anyone write that the long one was too short or the short one was too long? Did anyone say the long one was too long—but that she liked it anyway? If so, what was the reason?

91. Look for the 5 Ws

Wonder Woman is 2 Ws. The World Wide Web is 3 Ws. Nothing is 4 Ws.

But there is something that is 5 Ws—the big questions in journalism. Those questions are

- Who
- What
- Where
- When
- Why

In other words, who is the story about, what happened, where did it happen, when did it happen, and why did it happen?

Comb through a news story in the newspaper and see how quickly you find the 5 Ws. Do the same with a magazine article. The answers to the 5 questions don't always appear in the same order, or come early in the article—though many writers do try to get to them as soon as possible. See which article gives all 5 the quickest and which takes the longest to get to all 5.

92. Forge Your Own Armor

Ancient cultures fought a lot. (Then again, so do modern ones.)

The ancients used metals such as bronze to make armor and helmets. Make your own armor breastplate out of cardboard, aluminum foil, and string (and any other materials that are safe and handy).

1. Find a rectangular piece of cardboard big enough to cover your chest and stomach. You can cut out part of a large box, such as the kind a TV or large appliance comes in.

2. Completely wrap the cardboard in aluminum foil. You may need to use clear tape to secure it.

3. Hold the cardboard in front of you so that the 2 shorter ends are horizontal. Punch 2 holes in the top of the cardboard, one close to either corner.

4. Measure out enough string so it can hang around the back of your neck without being too tight, and tie each end through a hole.

5. You're left with a piece of cardboard that hangs comfortably around your neck and covers your chest and stomach perfectly.

If you're done but feel like you're just getting started, continue building your armor. Every body part needed protection, but you don't need to go that far. The helmet may be your greatest challenge since it requires eye and mouth slots.

Armor makes an impression, but knight after knight can start to look the same. There's a way to make your armor stand out. In books and online, look at various medieval emblems, insignias, and crests. Then design your own. Draw it on construction paper, cut it out, and tape it onto the breastplate.

Your armor won't suit you in battle, but it shouldn't have to.

No, this won't require you to give tag sales a score from 1 to 10.

Rather you'll run a tag sale in which all items are sold in terms of rates—for example, you might charge 50 cents per pound (0.5 kg) instead of 50 cents per item. Besides the items you will sell, all you'll need is a scale and a laundry basket.

Group items you're selling according to how much you want to sell them for and keep the groups on separate tables or in separate piles or boxes. You can divide by type of item; for example, all books can be a certain price per pound, as can all toys, clothes, and so forth. Make a sign for each group, such as "$1 per pound (0.5 kg)" or "25¢ per pound (0.5 kg)."

When a buyer has made his choices, weigh all items of the same price together (that is, weigh all the items from the dollar-per-pound (0.5 kg) table together, and so on). Then just subtract the weight of the laundry basket each time and add the cost of all the groups together to get the total amount the buyer owes.

94. Write to a Company

A company may seem like a large, impersonal thing, but of course it's made up of people.

Choose a company that you like. Maybe you like its products. Maybe you like its funny ad campaigns. Maybe you like it for supporting a charitable cause you also believe in. Maybe you just like its logo! Write that company a "fan letter" explaining what you like about it.

Or choose a company you've had a problem with and write a letter to it explaining why. Maybe you got a wireless keyboard as a gift but don't think it works very well, so you can let the company know by stating the facts.

You can find most company addresses online, and maybe even the right person to direct a letter or e-mail. If you write your letter with style, you may get a response—companies like to hear from customers, and the best ones write back to let you know that.

95. Tip the Waiter

Waiters work hard for their tips, and you'll have to work hard—and fast—to win this tip game.

Gather with friends around a table, each holding a small pad and a pencil. Choose one person to be the waiter. The waiter takes a few minutes to write down the amounts owed for the pretend meals everyone just ate. Each figure he makes up should be 4 digits, such as $18.02 or $67.13. It won't matter if some meals cost much more than others—as long as they're all 4 digits. How cheap or expensive each meal is won't give anyone an unfair advantage in what happens next.

The waiter walks around the table at a normal pace telling each person his individual charge, then starts around the table again. By the time he gets to each person the second time, everyone has to calculate the appropriate tip for his meal—and he has only 3 seconds once the waiter gets to him to say his tip. (It's a busy restaurant. No time to waste, but the more friends that play, the more time everyone will have to figure out the tip.) The tip amount is 20 percent. Diners can use knife-sharp minds and scrap paper, but no calculators.

However, the calculator ban does not apply to the waiter. He writes down each tip guess, then uses that calculator to see how close everyone is. Whoever is correct or the closest to correct becomes the waiter for the next round.

If you're playing with a bunch of math whizzes, you can change the tip amount each round, but it's realistic to keep it between 15 and 25 percent.

96. Rank a Book of Short Stories

The best short stories are so satisfying, you feel like you've just read a whole novel.

Read a book of short stories. Many are collections that have a common subject or theme, such as ghosts or growing up. Choose one that interests you. As you read each story, take brief notes and write down what you like and don't like.

When you're finished, rank the stories from the one you like the most to the one you like the least. You can also rank them individually on a scale of 1 to 5, 1 being a story you didn't like at all and 5 being a story you adored. Ask a sibling, friend, or parent to do the same and compare your rankings.

97. Create an Earthquake Map

When we look at a world map, everything looks calm.

But the Earth is a place that is constantly moving—and sometimes violently.

Get a world map (or print one out from the Web). Check books and Web sites to find the 10 largest earthquakes on record. Find the spot on the map where they occurred, and draw concentric circles for each one, one circle for each point on the Richter scale (the maximum—and most serious—is 10). For magnitudes ending in .5 or greater, round up. So, if a quake measured 6.4 on the Richter scale, you'll draw 6 concentric circles. If one measured 6.5, you'll draw 7 circles.

When you've marked all 10 quakes on the map, take another broad look. Does the world still look calm? Figure out the approximate distance between where you live and the nearest quake.

98. Tack on a Verse

Do you keep singing your favorite songs after they're done?

Give yourself a little more to sing by adding a verse (or more, if you want) to a song you love. Find the lyrics online if you don't have them from the CD booklet. Note the rhyme structure and number of syllables per line so your added verse fits in. You also want it to fit in thematically—if the song is about breaking up with a boyfriend, your verse should too.

Now when the song officially ends, your verse will keep it going unofficially, for a few measures anyway. If your sibling or friend tries this too, sing each other your new verse without playing the song it goes with and see who can guess what original song it comes from.

99. Jelly Bean Probability

Jelly beans are almost as famous for their colors as their flavors.

Get 30 jelly beans and record the color (or flavor) of each. Make sure you have a variety of flavors. Dump them all in a paper bag and ask a sibling or friend what chance he has to pull a particular flavor, then let him try.

Each time he picks a bean, he should adjust the probability of picking that one flavor. For example, if 7 out of the 30 jelly beans are cherry, you have a 7 in 30 chance of picking a cherry bean. If on the fifth try you finally pick a cherry, that means there are now 25 jelly beans left, of which 6 are cherry, so you have a 6 in 25 chance. If he should pick all cherry beans, he should switch to another flavor, keep picking, and crunch the numbers again.

After that, just munch the beans.

100. Asoka Says

Asoka was an emperor of India during the Maurya Dynasty (circa 265 B.C.E.) and was known for his good deeds. When he converted to Buddhism, he swore off violence (and meat).

This game is a variation on Simon Says. Someone refers to both a list of some of Asoka's benevolent deeds and a list of other benevolent deeds that Asoka did not do (though perhaps he would have if he'd thought of them).

Before starting the game, players can refresh their memories about Asoka by reading the first list— the one consisting of real Asoka deeds. Choose someone to be the caller. While the caller reads aloud a deed, one at a time, from one of the 2 lists (without saying which), everyone who thinks it was an Asoka deed shouts "Asoka!" (pronounced, according to Wikipedia, "a-shok-uh"). Those who are right remain in the game, those who are wrong are out. The winner is the last person still in the game.

Here are examples of what Asoka did do:

- Pursued peace with nearby states

- Tried to lessen poverty

- Built roads and wells

- Reduced the army

- Settled complaints among his people

- Forbid the killing of some animal species

Here are some possible red herrings, deeds Asoka did not explicitly do:

- Gave women equal rights as men

- Set the work week at three days

- Renamed the capital of India the Sanskrit word for "harmony"

- Freed all prisoners

- Donated his earnings to the poor

- Gave everyone unlimited health care

101. Host a Trivia Game Show

You may not have a studio or a wide selection of fabulous prizes, but you can run a game show just the same.

Dig up a bunch of facts, then write a bunch of trivia questions about them (either open-answer or fill-in-the-blank). Make sure your questions are as clear as they can be so the answers have less chance of being disputed. For example, if you write, "What is molten rock called?" there are 2 equally good answers—magma and lava. You'll have to specify "What is underground molten rock called?" if you're going for "magma" or "What is molten rock that has broken through the surface called?" if you're going for "lava."

Write at least 50 questions to have enough for a good game. As long as you don't mind being in the spotlight, host the show yourself, and call upon family and friends to be the contestants and audience members. Maybe you can even give away unwanted stuff from your room as prizes. . . .

102. Mode à la Mode

Have you ever noticed how ice cream is often white or cream-colored, even when its flavor is something more exotic, like lemon or banana or white chocolate chip?

To get the big picture, head to the freezer section of a supermarket or your favorite ice cream store. Write down the flavors of 20 common ice creams and their main color. Add up the total number of white or cream-colored ice creams; you'll probably see that this color is the most common mode, even when the flavor isn't just plain old vanilla.

Next write down how many times chocolate is part of the flavor mode, whether it's chocolate ripples or chips or candies, and add up the total. We bet you'll discover that chocolate "extras" are a popular ice cream mode, too.

Now it's time for you to choose your favorite flavor (common or uncommon), and enjoy a well-deserved treat!

103. Skim Something—Not Milk

See if you can understand a lot from a little.

Skim the first chapter of a book that you haven't read before and that you know nothing about—but skim in a specific way: Read just the first line of each paragraph in chapter 1. Then write a short summary of what you think that chapter is about. Reread the chapter in its entirety to see how close you were.

Do the same with a news story. Was one easier than the other to summarize this way, and, if so, why do you think that is? You can also do the same skim stunt with the last chapter of a book (but this is very challenging, and it's not recommended for a book you might want to read completely, since you'll be spoiling the ending).

104. Encyclopedia of You

You think you read a lot?

Aristotle (student of Plato, who was a student of Socrates) *really* read a lot. He studied literally dozens of subjects, including anatomy, astronomy, geography, geology, meteorology, physics, zoology; economics, ethics, government, politics, psychology, rhetoric, and theology; education, foreign customs, literature, and poetry. Makes your school workload look pretty good, huh? Aristotle helped develop the idea of an encyclopedia, a single book that explained lots of subjects.

Write an encyclopedia of the people, places, and objects in your life. Don't worry; it doesn't have to be 25 volumes long. Just choose at least 5 subjects and write encyclopedia-style entries for them. Refer to an encyclopedia to see an example of format. Examples of subjects: your school ("Norton Elementary School"), your street ("Stonehenge Place"), even your parents (Mom and Dad—but, in a nod to the formality of the encyclopedia, use their full names).

105. Well-Traveled Words

The English language incorporates lots of words from other languages.

1. Each time you read a book or article, jot down any words that sound foreign. When you want a break, look those words up in a dictionary and see if your hunch is right.

2. Check a dictionary or online dictionary for the origin of each word.

3. Keep building your list until you come across words from at least 3 languages besides English. For example, *hors d'oeuvres* (French), *angst* (German), or *quid pro quo* (Latin—it may be dead, but it's still a language).

You might not even realize that many common words or phrases that you use or hear all the time actually came from other languages—some examples are *gesundheit* (German) and *igloo* (Inuit). See how many you can find.

A lot of ingredients make up the guts of our planet.

Get a clear plastic container (Tupperware or, even better, a fishbowl—empty, of course). Decide what materials you'll use to represent the major levels of Earth—the crust, upper mantle, mantle, outer core, and inner core. Since the crust is cold and hard and the core is metallic, what can you use to represent the different textures? Possible materials include dirt, clay, crumpled aluminum foil, crumpled tissue paper, pebbles or gravel, even gelatin.

Fill the container, seal it airtight with a clear lid or thick piece of clear plastic and then tape it closed. Due to the nature of some of the materials, this may not be a permanent fixture.

107. Read Aloud

When it comes to written language, the eyes can be fooled but the ears can't.

Choose something you've written and edited, whether it's a story, an essay, or even a casual e-mail, and read it aloud. Do you come across any parts that don't sound as smooth when they're read out loud as they did when you wrote them? Does reading them out loud make you see right away how you can change them to make them better?

It's a good policy to read aloud your work, especially if it's something other people will be reading, such as a story you're sending to a magazine for possible publication. This is also good for homework assignments.

108. Whole Number Showdown

Being able to do math in your head is a valuable skill. So is good aim. And having both skills can make you a champion in this game.

Get a stack of 50 sticky notes. On each one, write a random 2-digit decimal number (3.4 or 9.1, for example), and don't repeat any. Stick all 50 notes to an outside wall in a big checkerboard grid, leaving about 2 inches (5 cm) between each. Compete with friends to add together as many pairs of decimal numbers to get whole numbers as you can—using a squirt gun.

Whoever is playing stands about 10 feet (3 m) away and gets 2 shots per turn. The goal is to hit 2 numbers that add up to a whole number, not a decimal

(for example, 6.2 + 1.8, which adds up to 8). Once a number has been hit, it can no longer be used in that particular game and can be taken down if players can't tell it's been hit. Keep in mind that not every number will be able to add with another to make a whole number, especially as you get toward the end of the game.

When you're done, add up your whole numbers—whoever has the most wins. Then let the notes dry (or rewrite them if need be) and play again.

109. Create a Web Site Flowchart

Every click on a Web site brings up something else. To get a better handle on how a Web site works, map out its inner workings.

1. You'll need a large piece of paper, or several large pieces of paper taped together, a colored pencil, and a good eraser.

2. Choose a theme for your Web site, a subject area that interests you and that you know something about. Let's use penguins for our example.

3. First draw your penguin home page: draw a huge square and add small boxes labeled with the standard commands "Back," "Next," and "Home."

4. Next add hyperlinks to your home page, which can also be represented by a row of small boxes. Let's say that your penguin home page needs at least 5 main hyperlinks: penguin types, penguin habitats, penguin life cycles, penguin FAQ, and one labeled "e-mail the Webmaster" (the Webmaster is you, in this case!).

5. Each of the first 4 hyperlinks should have arrows that lead to content: that's text, photographs, or both about the hyperlink topics. Maybe the penguin types page will lead to 3 more pages that describe king, emperor, and Adélie penguins. The penguin life cycles link might lead to separate pages that discuss birth, early years, mating, and death and show pictures of a penguin in each stage.

6. Don't worry if the arrows in your flowchart begin to curve off in crazy directions. Just be sure that your hyperlink boxes are clearly connected by arrows to the relevant content.

7. Once you have filled in all your content descriptions, test out your flowchart on a friend or parent. Ask them if they can get from your home page to information about penguins' early years by following the arrows in your chart.

8. If your test run reveals glitches in your Web site, don't worry, you drew your chart in pencil so you can easily erase and revise it.

9. For an extra challenge, consider researching the content outlined in your flowchart thoroughly, then posting your site on the Web. If you've never done this before, ask an adult or computer savvy friend to help you out.

110. Fraction Concentration

There is a way to have twice as much fun from a fraction of an idea.

It's a game similar to Concentration (sometimes called Memory), only done with fractions. Get 20 index cards. Ask a sibling or friend to write one fraction on each card. The fractions must form 10 pairs—a fraction and its most simplified form such as $^{15}/_{24}$ and $^{5}/_{8}$. Ask someone else to double-check all the cards to make sure each card has only one possible match. For example, your set of 20 couldn't include $^{3}/_{4}$, $^{9}/_{12}$, and $^{12}/_{16}$ because both $^{9}/_{12}$ and $^{12}/_{16}$ can be reduced to $^{3}/_{4}$.

Shuffle the cards and lay them face down on a table or the floor. Then proceed like Concentration—take turns with a sibling or friend, overturning 2 cards at a time, trying to find a match. If you do, keep the cards and go again. If you don't, turn the cards back over and let the next player try. Whoever has the most cards at the end of the game wins. If 20 cards gets too easy, make more!

111. Practice Your Parthian Shot

In the Persian kingdom of Parthia, archers learned to shoot a bow and arrow backward—while on horseback.

See how good your aim is from a similar position. Challenge a sibling or friend to a Parthian tournament. Ball up a bunch of pieces of scrap paper or old newspapers—these are your substitute arrows. Walk briskly away from a trash can, turn back while continuing to walk, and throw a balled-up piece of paper toward the can. Take turns doing this 10 times in a row and see who gets more "hits" (that is, baskets).

To make sure you're both tossing your wad of paper at approximately the same distance, place a piece of tape on the floor or ground; when you reach it, that's when you throw.

112. Design a Renewable Logo

We can renew more than library books and magazine subscriptions.

The U.S. Department of Agriculture has a label for organic food. That label means the food has not been grown or prepared with chemicals.

Just as organic food is good for both us and the environment, so are renewable resources, which are natural energy sources that replenish themselves over time. Unlike organic food, however, they're usually not for sale at the supermarket.

Renewable resources include the following:

- Wind energy
- Solar energy

Renewable materials include the following:

- Wood

- Air

- Leather

- Water (okay, this one is for sale at the supermarket)

Pretend that the rest of these types of energy sources were bottled and sold in stores, and design a logo for them. The only requirement is that it must contain the words "renewable material." Your label will serve as a reminder to people to respect the Earth, because we have only one. Enough pressure for you?

113. Write a Comic Strip

Comic strips are proof that small things can deliver big laughs.

Make one of your own—maybe you'll make yourself giggle. Your comic strip can be made of 1, 2, 3, or 4 boxes. It must have words and it should be your best shot at being funny. (Otherwise it's not a comic strip but just a strip!) This is not just about the drawing but equally about the writing. In the best comic strips, the art works with the text to tell the joke, and if you were to remove one or the other, nobody would get it.

Before you create your own comic strip, look at the comic strips in the newspaper for a few days to see how they're written and how they are set up. Are the jokes usually in the first panel, the middle one, or the last? Do different characters have different ways of talking? Are some comic strips heavy with text, even though the space is small? Using all of this information, plan your characters (your own, please!) and think of the situation that will lead to your joke.

114. One Mean Family

There's a mean in every family.

Not a mean person—a mathematical mean.

Figure out the mean age of your family by adding together all your ages, then dividing by the number of people included. You can do this for immediate family, meaning whoever lives with you, then include extended family like grandparents, uncles, aunts, and cousins. You can even include pets if you want—but for any dogs, use human years, not dog years.

Then host a casual quiz show in which your family must guess what the family's mean age is from a choice of 3 that you write on pieces of construction paper. Continue the game by having them guess the means of different groups within the family (which you will have computed in advance), such as the mean age of all grandparents or all cousins.

115. Read Your Parents' Writing

Whatever age you are, your parents once were the same age, too.

However different you think you and your parents are now, here's a way to see if you are similar to their younger selves.

Go on a quest to find some of their work from when they were in grade school. Or if it's not so easy to find, just ask them if they remember where their old papers are. With any luck, they saved some of their old schoolwork or letters, and would be happy for you to read it. If you're successful in finding some, compare their writing to your own—both what they wrote and the handwriting itself. Does is seem like any of their interests or activities were similar to yours? Can you tell that you are your parents' child?

116. Earthquake versus Volcano

Shark versus Lion. Alien versus Vampire. Your Fourth-Grade Teacher versus your Fifth-Grade Teacher.

These are monumental battles that will probably never happen, but that doesn't mean you can't imagine an outcome if they did. Here's one you can sort of figure out: earthquakes versus volcanoes? Guess first, then get the facts.

Create a comparison chart between the 2 formidable forces of nature, charting the number of active volcanoes versus the number of active fault lines in the world. Then look up how many earthquakes took place between the years 1900 and 2000 and compare it to the number of volcanic eruptions during the same period. To make the rivalry even bigger, find out whether there are earthquakes and/or volcanoes on other planets. Mars-quakes, anyone?

117. Study People Talking

You may think we all speak in perfect sentences, one clearly phrased sentence after the other, just like in some books.

Some of us do. But the truth is, well, many people don't speak, like, you know, the way they do in books, meaning the way they are written to speak in books. They speak like that last sentence—in spurts, correcting themselves, going on too long, and using words like "well," "uh," and "um" a lot. After all, we're not using scripts. Every sentence we say is complete improv.

Spend an afternoon paying close attention to how people really talk. Sit on the playground or some other location with lots of people and listen. Take notes and you'll quickly hear the evidence. As a side experiment, note what kind of people speak the most fluidly—meaning with the least amount of "speed bumps" like "er" and "eh" and other "words" that never get asked during spelling bees. Is it young people like you, people your parents' age (yes, that old), or elderly people (yes, really old)? Do you notice if it's more male or female?

Then rewrite every choppy sentence you've written down in a way it could appear in a book. You want to keep the meaning—but get to it quicker!

When writing original dialogue for your own stories, strive to make it seem real without being too real, which would, believe it or not, get annoying to read. By listening to real "dialogue," you'll help yourself improve the authenticity of your story dialogue. You'll learn how to imitate real language while leaving out the words that get in the way.

118. Han Me a Gong

During the Han Dynasty in China (202 B.C.E. to 220 C.E.), people used gongs as instruments during military expeditions.

Make a gong of your own. You need a piece of metal (round is ideal) and something to bang against it. If you use the lid of one of your parents' pots or pans or a garbage can lid, get permission first. Before you were born, there was a TV game show called *The Gong Show*—a silly talent contest in which participants were gonged if they were so bad the judges couldn't bear to let them go on. You could host a gong show of your own! Friends provide the talent acts (or talentless acts, as the case may be), and you can be the master gonger.

119. Separate Fact from Fiction

Historical fiction is a blend of the 2 main book categories. You're going to unblend them.

Read any book of historical fiction. Do some research to find out what is real and what has been made up for the story. A character may be based on a real person, but an event that person witnesses may be fictional. Or a fictional character may be inserted into an actual moment in history. If the book contains an author's note that explains what is fact and what is fiction, don't refer to it until after you've poked around on your own. You'll feel especially accomplished if you predict what it says.

120. The Origin of Myths

You've heard of the Cyclops, the legendary giant with one eye?

One theory behind that larger-than-life myth is that people found an elephant skull and thought it had come from a one-eyed giant (they mistook the socket of the trunk for a single, large eye socket).

Make up a believable explanation for another creature that appeared in Greek mythology, such as the siren (part woman, part bird), the centaur (half human, half horse), Pegasus (a winged horse) or the Sphinx (part lion, eagle, and human). Write descriptive text and illustrate it with drawings of the mythical creature. If you're especially ambitious, make an entire myth-busting mini-book, exposing the "truths" behind as many Greek myths as you can.

121. Ten Percent Up!

Don't say "Gimme five." Go for 10!

With a sibling or friend, start a simple neighborhood business, such as a yardwork service, computer lessons, dog walking, or car washing. Set a goal to increase business by 10 percent every week (or month) of the summer. So, if you make $50 one week, you'll need to make $55 the next (because 10 percent or .10 x $50 = $5, and $50 + $5 = $55).

While you'll need math to check if you're meeting your goal, you'll need something else to actually meet the goal: marketing. Spreading good word of mouth about your business will probably have the most influence on raising your profits. Also, come up with a clever promotion that makes your new business irresistible. If you offer computer lessons for $10 per hour, give your clients the option to e-mail you an additional question afterward for no charge. Or if you're walking dogs for $5 per dog and a client has more than one dog, offer a 10 percent discount for each additional dog. There's that number again!

There is a phenomenon we can call "Reverse Expectations." This is when we love something we expect to loathe and loathe something we expect to love.

Test this phenomenon the next time you choose your next read.

If you (think you) hate comic books, go to the comic book store and poke around until you find one that may interest you.

If you (think you) dislike political articles, get a copy of *Time for Kids* or *Teen Newsweek* and read an article about current events.

If you (think you) are instantly bored by biographies, find one that got great reviews—even if it's about someone you don't think you're interested in, even if it's a picture book—and read it.

If you (think you) don't get poetry, check out poetry books in the library and thumb through till you find a poem that not only makes sense to you but intrigues you too.

Keep doing this until you find an exception to every type of material you supposedly don't like to read. You'll see that sometimes you only think you don't like something. . . .

How could this happen? How could something you think you know about yourself be proven wrong? You may not like poetry, but you may love cars. If you find a poem about cars, the car part may overcome the poetry part. Or if you like computers but don't care for biographies, you may still enjoy the biography of the guy who is credited with creating the World Wide Web.

123. Go on an Adjective Diet

Write a description about something that has inspired you or means something to you in some way, such as a person, a place, or an event.

But do it using as few adjectives as possible. Get your points across using similes and metaphors. Both are ways to make something new out of language rather than reuse words many other writers use. For example, if you're writing about a cabin your family goes to in the summer, don't call it "small and cozy." Instead, try something more colorful.

Here's a simile: "The cabin always feels like a squirrel's den, except there's barely any room to store nuts." This conveys that the cabin is small—cramped, actually. Similes compare things, usually using the words "like" or "as."

Here's a metaphor: "The cabin is a living room fort with walls of wood instead of blankets." This can convey small, but cozy. Metaphors also compare 2 things, but without "like" or "as." Usually, metaphors describe one thing as another as if they're the same.

You'll find that trying to think of similes and metaphors will automatically decrease the number of adjectives you use.

124. Find New Language

Language can grow faster than people do!

Ten years ago, did you know what a blog was? Or a trans fat? Or CGI? Or phat?

Read an article in a newspaper or magazine about a subject that interests you. As you do, circle any words that you think—or know—have entered the language fairly recently. Then confirm by checking a dictionary that lists the first known occurrence of every word. Can you think of 5 other words that are new? If you have trouble, try thinking in terms of entertainment, technology, and health, 3 areas where knowledge—and language—is constantly growing.

You can also contribute to our ever-changing language. Maybe you think a person who responds too slowly to e-mail could be called an e-snail. See if your word catches on by continuing to scan the newspaper . . . maybe your word will show up there!

125. Build a Mini-Tomb

For ancient Egyptians, the end of life was the beginning of the afterlife. And some didn't exactly pack light for it.

Refresh your memory about what privileged ancient Egyptians put in their burial tombs and make a small version of your own—too small for you, of course! If you have a yard and your parents agree, dig a small hole and fill it with homemade versions of what the Egyptians used, kind of like an outdoor diorama. If you don't have a yard or your parents say no digging, use a shoebox like a standard diorama.

You'll need to make a miniature version of a sarcophagus (a stone coffin in the shape of the enclosed mummy) and possibly a table, a chest of jewelry, statues, a book of prayers, jewels, or even a mummified pet, among other things.

126. Hide the Epicenter

You and some friends can get to the bottom of fun by finding the center of things.

1. Make up a place and draw a simple map of it—after it's been shaken by an earthquake.

2. Indicate the epicenter and the various towns and natural and manmade formations nearby, such as rivers, mountains, dams or airports.

3. Indicate how damaged each of them were using a scale of 1 to 10, with 1 being not damaged and 10 being the most damaged. Generally, the closer it is to the epicenter, the more damage an area suffers.

4. In a yard or large room, "re-create" the area you mapped on a larger scale by writing each map location on its own small index card and laying each on the ground in roughly the same position as it appears on the map.

5. Place a small marker (such as a dime or a button) on the epicenter, but make sure that it can't be seen unless someone looks very closely.

6. Give family or friends the map and ask them to use it to locate the epicenter (which won't be labeled, just like it's not in real life).

7. If your "seismologists" don't find the epicenter, you can reveal how close they got to it.

127. Make Your House a DEAR One

Your home is surely already sweet, but is it DEAR?

Suggest that your family commit to a day once a week to Drop Everything and Read. This is a surprise event that anyone in the family can kick off just by shouting "DEAR!" The call should go out when the whole family is home and doing things other than talking on the phone, sleeping, or anything time-sensitive. When everyone else hears the call, they stop what they're doing and read for 20 minutes. It can be a book, newspaper, or magazine—not the back of the cereal box. If someone can't stop at that moment, it's up to him to call out DEAR at a time more convenient for him within the next 24 hours. At your next family meal, discuss what you've all read.

128. Make a Movie Poster

In between watching summer blockbuster movies, design a poster for one.

It can be for a real movie or one you make up. Most posters don't have many words, but that doesn't mean the text is easy to write. These posters are designed to get you to invest your money and about 2 hours of your time using only an image and a few words. Those have to be clever words! Study some current movie posters to get ideas—you can find them at your local cinema, on billboards, in magazine ads, and online (search "movie posters"). Of course, this activity involves drawing, too, but don't worry—the words count more here.

If your siblings and friends do the same, hang them up as a "movie-poster gallery" and vote for which movie of the bunch you'd be most likely to see based only on its poster.

129. Make Your Room a Museum

Museums are great, but they have their drawbacks: they're not open all the time, they're often crowded, and you can never touch the exhibits. Plus you can't strut around in your underwear.

Those rules won't necessarily apply when you create a museum in your very own bedroom.

Choose a historical era you like and make several exhibits based on it. If you focus on ancient Egypt, you can have a papier-mâché (or even Lego) pyramid, a large piece of paper showing the Sphinx's eye at actual size, a computer presentation on hieroglyphs, and so on. Make your exhibits diverse. You don't want everything to be a drawing—that won't generate rave reviews.

Clear off your desk, bureau, and other flat surfaces. (Your parents now officially love this activity.) Decide how you're going to arrange your exhibit. Will you have a countertop for different aspects of an era, such as clothes, food, or religious beliefs? Will everything be arranged randomly?

Use a computer to create small explanatory signs for each artifact or item. On each sign, write what the item is, what year or period it is from, and anything unusual about it. Of course, you can make this up, but base it on the kind of thing you might really read on a museum sign. Prop, tape, or stand the signs along their corresponding items.

Add detail to your museum in other ways. Perhaps your family has an old glass aquarium you can use as a case for one of your more valuable specimens. Maybe you can even convince a friend to dress up like a security guard and stand at the entrance (meaning your door).

When you're ready for visitors, invite people to the grand opening of your museum. Should you charge admission? Only if you think you can get away with it.

130. Compare News Stories

The news is factual, but different reporters may interpret facts differently.

Get 3 different daily newspapers. Pick a big story of the week and read the article about it in each publication. (Since it is a big story, they'll all have an article on it, guaranteed.) Pay attention to what information appears in all 3 articles, what information appears in 2 but not the third, and what information appears in only one. Do you find any discrepancies or different facts among the articles? Does any article seem more trustworthy than the others?

Then go multimedia. Compare your newspaper stories to the same story on the TV news and on a major news Web site.

By now, 3 things will have happened:

1. You'll know the facts of this story by heart, backward and forward. You may be close to becoming an expert on the issue. Maybe they'll even call you for a quotation for a follow-up story.

2. You'll form an opinion about the story in general. What's more, you'll have an opinion about which source told the story the best.

3. Your eyes will be tired.

Make a comparison chart about facts mentioned, checking off which source mentions which facts.

131. Write a Modern Epic Poem

Not all poems are short and rhyming.

Some are long and don't rhyme at all, but tell the story of great quests or important events. These are called epics. A few thousand years ago, the breathless adventures related in the great Greek epic poems *The Iliad* and *The Odyssey* may have been as popular in their day as blockbuster movies are in ours.

Tap into that excitement by choosing a more recent book you love and rewriting it in epic-poem form. But to get in the mood and to get the feel for this type of epic poetry, first read Homer's epic poems. Your library probably has several versions. And when you get to writing, just summarize your story—don't even try to make your poem as long as the original!

132. Cold Pizza

Regular pizza tastes just as good in summer, but "cold pizza" tastes even better.

With a parent's help, make 3 cold personal-sized pizzas by topping large plain cookies with ice cream or pudding as the cheese and frozen berries or other deliciously cold things as the extra toppings. And make each pizza "fractionally," the way pizzerias often do—say, top ¼ with M&Ms, ¼ with blueberries, and ½ with strawberries.

Make different combinations for all 3 pizzas. Then see how much a sibling or friend knows about fractions by asking him questions based on your mini-pizza trio. Which pizza is ⅓ whip-cream topped, ¼ Skittles? Then, of course, eat your hard work.

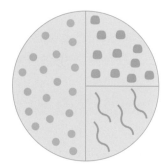

133. The Strength of Sound Waves

Round up a radio, several CDs, and a tape recorder or digital voice recorder. Put all of it in a room and close the door.

Have a sibling or friend stand outside the door and down the hall. Call to him when you're about to turn on a sound at a fairly low volume level. Your friend writes down what he hears, if anything (is it a song, a voice, a recording of a dog barking, static, or some other sound?). Then tell him to take a few steps closer to the door and repeat—for every position he moves to, you play the same sound at the same volume level and he jots down what he hears.

Now try the experiment with the door open, then with the door closed again but the volume louder or softer, and observe how the results vary in each case. How close was your sound partner before he knew without a doubt what he was hearing?

134. Write a Script for a Silent Show

Hollywood writers make big bucks. See if you have what it takes.

Choose a sitcom you like and tape an episode that you haven't seen. Then watch it—with the sound turned off. Based on what you think happened from the visuals alone, write a script to go along with it.

Watch the show again with the sound on and see if any of your script's elements overlap with—or are even funnier than—the actual show. This is best done with a short show, even a cartoon.

Finally, invite friends over, turn the sound down again, pass out copies of your script, assign roles, and put on a weird new type of play. If your writing itself isn't hilarious, maybe your friends' acting will be.

135. Keep a Thunderstorm Log

Weather wizards say that thunderstorms are most common in summer. See if they're right when it comes to your region.

Keep track of the thunderstorms that pass through in June, July, and August. Write down approximately when each storm starts and how long it lasts, and if the rain is accompanied by thunder and/or lightning. If a storm hits at night, don't stay up to measure its duration—in that case, noting just the date is enough. If possible, note how many seconds elapse between the flicker of lightning and the boom of thunder—does it get longer or shorter over the course of the storm? If you have a rain gauge, place it in an unobstructed area of your yard (if you live in an apartment you can put it on the fire escape—just make sure the rain won't be blocked by the eaves of your roof) and record the amount of rain you get each day in inches or centimeters.

The next day, check the newspaper to find out if any damage was caused by the storm. At season's end, compare all the storms—and if you're ambitious, continue the log from September to May to see if summer really is the season of thunderstorms.

136. Find Reliable Sources

Primary and secondary sources are the ingredients of any top-notch research project.

Say you're doing research on the civil rights movement for an assignment or a short story you're writing. Get online and start searching. Copy and paste all the URLs (Web site addresses) about the civil rights movement into a Word document and indicate whether you'd consider them primary, secondary, or unreliable sources for facts.

Primary sources are documents that include eyewitness, firsthand accounts of an event (for example, a letter written by Martin Luther King, Jr., describing his philosophy of nonviolent resistance, or a transcript of an interview with a person who participated in a Birmingham, Alabama, sit-in). Good places to start looking for primary sources would be the Web sites of official, respected institutions; for example, the Library of Congress's African American Odyssey Web page has links to primary sources about the civil rights movement.

Secondary sources are books, articles, essays, and other documents that either gather research from multiple primary sources or that don't deal directly with an event the author participated in. Most books and magazine and newspaper articles are secondary sources, as are Web sites of popular history and social studies magazines and journals, like *American Heritage*. You can also try Web sites of large and small institutions that you may not have heard of and even some well-written private sites if the person's credentials and sources are listed. The Civil Rights Division of the Department of Justice has a Web site that describes the laws relating to civil rights in the United States—these summaries are secondary sources.

Unreliable sources are usually badly written, unsubstantiated, or factually contradictory to what at least 3 of your primary or secondary sources state. They often look sloppy, too!

137. Write Fortunes for Cookies

Confucius (circa 551–479 B.C.E.) was a Chinese philosopher whose short phrases of wisdom sometimes appear on those little slips inside fortune cookies.

"People who do not plan for the future will have trouble near at hand" is one example. "If you disagree with your parents, admonish them gently" is another. Can you do better?

Come up with 10 fortunes that you think:
(1) are legitimate fortunes that have something to do with the future and **(2)** will be so encouraging that the recipients will hang them on their fridge. Then stick them in various cookies—not only fortune cookies—and distribute them to friends and family. For example, bake chocolate chip cookies and fold them over while still hot (use a glove!) so they'll cool into a sandwich-type shape. Then insert fortunes in them.

138. Activity for a Rainy Day

Summer sunshine gets most of the praise, but a light summer rain can be very refreshing.

Sunny days usually outnumber rainy days anyway . . . or do they?

Create bar graphs of daily rainfall from the first day of summer vacation to the last—one bar graph each for the months of June, July, and August. Along the horizontal border, list the days of the month, and along the vertical border, list the rainfall in inches or centimeters.

The day before school starts, see how many days were rainy and what the total summer rainfall was. You can then see if your family and friends paid attention to the rain patterns. Cover up the word "rainfall" and show them your graphs. Ask if they think the graphs are charting daily high temperature, price of a gallon or liter of gas, box office gross, or rainfall.

139. One Glass, One Temperature

Heat likes to move, and it doesn't need a dance floor to do it.

This movement is called *heat flow*. Get a large glass and 2 smaller glasses. Fill one of the smaller glasses with cold water and the other with boiling water (with adult supervision). Use a thermometer to take the temperature of each. Pour equal amounts of water from each small glass into the larger glass, stir, and check its temperature. Is it halfway between the cold and hot temperatures? Or does cold or hot seem more "dominant" after the 2 are mixed?

140. Ride a Magic Carpet

Well, there's magic and a carpet. . . .

Tell a friend you have a magic carpet in your house, and when you stand on it, you can perform magic. Show him the magic carpet, (and to prove it) ask your friend in his head to:

1. Think of a number between 2 and 9
2. Multiply that number by 9
3. Add the 2 digits of the answer together
4. Subtract 5

For example, if your friend picked 8, he would multiply it by 9 [8 x 9 = 72], then add those digits together [7 + 2 = 9], then subtract 5 [9 – 5 = 4].

Then tell your friend:

5. Figure out which letter corresponds to that number if 1 = A, 2 = B, and so on
6. Think of a country that begins with that letter
7. Think of an animal that begins with the next letter

First do the magic number trick when you're not standing on the carpet—and get it wrong. Say something like, "A squid in Russia? How bizarre!"

Then step onto the carpet. Repeat the trick. Once that's done, look very deeply at your friend and say, "An elephant in Denmark? Works every time.

Our brains may be more powerful than you realize: We can slitl raed wdors eevn if msot of the lrtetes hvae been jbemuld up.

The olny leertts taht msut saty in tiehr raguler pcaels are the fsirt and lsat oens. Eevn wehn the ohtres are ceemopllty out of oedrr, you wlil siltl uaednnrstd the mnanieg of the stecenne. The raoesn for tihs cloud be taht our hamun mdnis do not raed ecah ltteer by iesltf. Isetnad, it tkeas in the wrod as a wohle.

Try writing a sentence like this and see if a sibling or friend can umnslabcre it in his head.

142. Race in a Mathathon

All races involve calculation—otherwise the runners wouldn't know how fast they were.

Ask a parent, sibling, or friend who is good at math to create between 20 and 40 math problems, each on its own index card. They can be any kind you agree on, but not too easy.

Create a race route in a parent-approved location, such as a backyard or park. It doesn't need to be long because there's a twist—your math maestro will place the index cards at certain spots along the race route, one set of cards in each spot for each competitor. In other words, if 3 people will be racing, each "math stop" will have 3 cards. When you get to a math stop, you must figure out the answer to your math problem and write it on the card.

At the end of the race, there may be multiple winners—whoever came across the finish line first and whoever got the most math problems correct. Or they may both be you!

143. Pick up the Details

Even people who love to read don't remember everything they've read.

See if the same phenomenon applies if a person is being read to rather than reading himself. Read the opening paragraphs or first pages of 3 well-written books to a sibling or friend, then see how well she listened. Tell her to close her eyes. Randomly read a short, interesting phrase from one of the 3 passages you read and ask if she remembers which book it was from.

For (even more) fun, throw in a few phrases that you made up in advance that don't appear in *any* of the opening paragraphs. If it's still too easy, do this with 4—or 5 or 6—books.

144. Write around Something

Good writing is about using words in a descriptive way.

Write a short story about someone or something—a dog, a robot, a sumo wrestler, or anything else that interests you—but don't use the noun that describes that certain someone or something. What are other ways you can convey that a dog is a dog without saying so?

This challenge applies not just to the first mention of the character but to the whole story! You could write,

"It looked like a metal pretzel with dents instead of pieces of salt. The pedals were crusty with dirt and the handlebars had lost their shine." This passage doesn't spell out what it's describing, but did it put an image in your head? Did it make you think of a bike?

145. Knee-High Landslide

Large landslides can be caused by various factors, from rain to earthquakes. They're unpredictable and terrifying.

Small landslides can be caused by you—and they're the opposite of unpredictable and terrifying.

In a yard, simulate a landslide in which no one can possibly get hurt—though you will get dirty! That is because you will start by getting dirt.

Use buckets to collect a variety of soils and rocks. Choose a location on grass, pavement, or dirt and build your own mini-mountain. Just as dirt inside the house may annoy your parents, dirt outside it can, too—so ask their permission to use your chosen site before you begin.

Pile the materials up into a mountain shape. If it helps you keep it together, use water to pack the dirt and rocks into a shape that does not instantly crumble. It should be at least knee-high, but go higher if you've got the materials and the desire. (If you end up reaching the height of a real mountain, you've gone way too far.) Stick a toothpick or a flag in the top. Take a picture of your peak.

Let it be until it rains. Once the showers have passed, you should find that your mountain has changed. If it's not completely washed away, it may leave evidence of a mini-landslide. Some heavy materials that were at the top may have tumbled down to the bottom, just as they do in large-scale landslides.

Bonus bargain bonanza: in learning about landslides, you're also getting a gravity lesson thrown in at no additional charge to you.

146. Calculate Average Car Speed

You may be too young to drive, but you don't need a license to collect data about how other people drive.

Call the local police station (*not* the emergency number) and explain that you want to do a project in which you monitor the speed of passing cars on your street for an hour; they may be willing to help you. If not, set up a table in a safe place on the side of your road (or the safest nearby road, if you live on a main road or a road with no sidewalks). Prop up a large sign saying, "Youth Project: Your Speed Tracked Today—Please Stop and Share." And if that doesn't work, try bribery—offer free lemonade (again with a prominent sign). Motorists may be too busy to stop for a survey, but not for a drink!

Gather as many speeds as you can to figure out the average speed on your street, which will hopefully be at or below the speed limit. If it's not, report your findings to the police. They may be able to install new signs, speed bumps, or some other form of speeding deterrent.

147. Read a Movie

We always say we "saw" a movie, but before any movie is watchable, it's readable.

Ask a librarian to help you find some screenplays. Try reading 2—one of a film you've seen and one of a film you haven't.

After the second one, rent the film. How does the movie compare to the script? Also, what do you find missing in screenplays that you would find in a regular book? And do screenplays have any components that books don't have?

As an added challenge, try converting a short scene from a book you like to screenplay format. You'll use fewer words—but do you think that makes it easier to write?

148. Photograph Heat and Cold

It's so unoriginal to photograph solid things. Everyone does that!

Instead, capture degrees on film—images that give an idea of the temperature. Try to get at least one photograph of shimmering heat waves coming off pavement and another of frosty breath or air. That second one could be tricky in summer, but there are ways to do it if you're creative (think: freezer).

And getting back to solids, what else can you photograph that indicates the temperature in a more abstract way? Instead of taking a picture of someone in a pool (which suggests hot), try a close-up of a forehead dotted with sweat or something melting (which also suggest hot). For cold companion photos, you'll probably have to find a heavily air-conditioned place or wait till winter. Get creative about those as well, and see what you can come up with.

149. Go Metric for a Day

Back before you (and Web conversion calculators) were born, some Americans tried to convince their country to switch to the metric system.

They didn't succeed . . . but get prepared in case they try again and do better. For one day, keep track of the measurements of everything you use or do and convert each figure/amount to metric. If you drink an 8-ounce bottle of water, convert it to the metric equivalent (that's an easy one, since the metric measurement is also printed on the label). Weigh yourself and convert that number to kilograms. Race your friends in the 50-yard dash, then compute how many meters that is.

If you watch a DVD on your family's 27-inch TV . . . if your mom drives you to the pool at 30 miles per hour . . . and no matter how hot it feels in Fahrenheit, convert that to Celsius and the lower number may take the edge off.

150. Make a Monster

Books are safe places to keep monsters, don't you think?

Find a book that has a description—but no illustrations—of some kind of monster that is generally unfamiliar. A good source for this is mythology, particularly a myth from another country or an ancient culture.

Read just that description aloud to a group of friends and have them on paper draw their interpretation of the monster. Then compare each other's work. If the drawings are all similar, does that mean the description was good?

You can then look in other books, or online, to see if you can find other artists' interpretations of that particular creature.

151. Compare an Original to a Sequel

Some things get better with practice.

Write an article comparing 2 books or 2 movies that feature the same characters—with books, think series, and with movies, think sequels.

Consider the various aspects of a book (characters, plot, pace, writing style) or film (characters, plot, acting, music, cinematography). Does the second book or movie improve upon the first in any way, does it get worse than the first, or is it just as successful? Compare the strengths and weaknesses of the pair you have chosen.

In the end, if one is better than the other, describe why you think so.

152. Tests You Can't Study For

A major soft drink company once held a "blind taste test" in which people were asked to taste two competing brands of soda and say which they liked better—without knowing which soda was in which cup. Why stop at taste?

Here are some other sense tests you can try with your friends.

Blind Smell Test: Only the bravest noses need apply. Have your friends sit in a circle and remove one sock. Put all socks in a bag and pass the bag around. Everyone must pull one sock from the bag and identify whose it is—with eyes closed—by smell alone.

Blind Sight Test: Ask a group of friends to draw their self-portraits . . . you guessed it—with their eyes closed. Hang the drawings up and ask them to identify the artist-subject of each masterpiece. Also acceptable: draw the self-portrait with eyes open—but use your nondominant hand. In other words, right-handed people must draw with their left, and vice versa.

Blind Hearing Test: Record a few friends singing the chorus to your favorite rock song, one at a time and with no one beside you in the room. (Also, make sure they don't know the order in which you recorded them.) Gather them together, play each rendition on the "slow" or "fast" speed, and ask them to guess whose version is whose.

Blind Touch Test: Get 3 small bowls and (with a parent's permission) fill one with pudding, one with yogurt, and one with Jello. Ask your friends to stick a (clean) finger in each, and try to tell which is which simply by the *feel* of it—and no finger licking.

153. Submit to a Magazine

Editors out there want to hear from you.

Some magazines publish work by young people: stories, essays, poems, drawings, and photos. Never heard this? Don't believe it? Visit the Stone Soup Web site, which lists the names and Web sites of real magazines that publish real kids' work, and also the kind of submissions they're looking for.

Find one that seems to fit you and give it a go. It only costs a little bit of time and a little bit of postage. Just don't send out the first draft of whatever you do—revise it until you feel it's as good as you can make it. Even when you think you're done, first try putting it aside for a week without looking at it. Sometimes that time away makes you see your words in a whole new way.

For some people, the most exciting time is waiting to hear from an editor—a phone call with good news could come at any minute! If you start now, by the end of summer vacation you may be on your way to being a published writer.

154. Host a Backyard Olympics

The ancient Greeks contributed much to world civilization, including the Olympic Games. Host your own!

Encourage family, friends, and friendly neighbors to get their game on. Some events you can run without need of a stadium: the 66-yard (60-meter sprint), the relay race (the number of participants is up to you and the distance depends on how much space you have), the discus throw (a Frisbee is an acceptable substitute), swimming races if you have a pool, and the long jump.

Don't feel the need to pay tribute to the ancient Olympics down to the last detail. For one thing, back then athletes were all male and competed in the nude!

155. Edit a Neighborhood Newsletter

Local newspapers can cover only so much.

Create a newsletter about the goings-on of the street you live on or the building or complex you live in and distribute it to neighbors.

You may think there's nothing worth writing about, but do a little investigative reporting and you'll probably find that everyone has a cool story. You can profile people who live there. You can do a story on events they're involved in or events that have happened on the street—especially exciting ones that people may not have heard about. Maybe a neighbor is in the process of adopting a baby from China? Or maybe that elderly woman across the street was a beauty pageant winner in her youth? People love to read about stuff like that.

Name the newsletter, write a few stories (and even ask family and neighborhood friends if they want to write any), and include a few original photos and illustrations. Photocopy or print out copies and stick them in mailboxes or distribute them in whatever other way works.

156. Ad Analysis

Ads are often about visual literacy—making quick associations between an image and a product. Sometimes the product being sold is not even shown!

Count every full-page advertisement in the latest issue of your favorite magazine. How many pages of the magazine are ads as opposed to content? What percentage of total pages is that?

Make a bar graph with each of the following questions answered:

1. How many ads advertise food?

2. How many have only one line of text?

3. How many advertise books?

4. How many are funny?

5. How many are trying to be funny?

6. How many involve animals?

7. How many caught your eye when you looked through the magazine the first time?

Add your own questions too, if you want.

157. Keep Score Askew

The game will be the same, but the score will take more brain power.

With friends, choose a game that scores with points (such as baseball). But instead of the usual score-keeping method, create a new system—and it must be based on fractions. For example, with baseball, assign $\frac{1}{2}$ point for a home run, $\frac{1}{3}$ point for reaching home from first, $\frac{1}{4}$ point for reaching home from second, and $\frac{1}{5}$ point for reaching home from third.

Or you can be more generous—a home run is $4\frac{1}{2}$ points, reaching home from first earns $3\frac{3}{5}$ points, and so on. And don't use only fractions involving halves—that's too easy.

Play through the game, and see what kind of final score you end up with.

158. Make Science Word Puzzles

Science is about breaking things down to understand the big picture.

Make a list of various things you've studied in science (insects, computers, rainforests, layers of the earth, whatever the case may be), and look at their various parts.

Write the names of the major parts of each thing on separate index cards or same-sized slips of paper. Take "insect," for example: you'd write head, thorax, abdomen, antennae, and so on. Then mix the cards together and try to "rebuild" each thing by dividing the cards into corresponding groups. The more items you break down, the more challenging your fun will be.

A bizarro bonus: mix-and-match the various parts and draw a picture of the monster you've created.

159. Make a Fountain of Youth

You're never too young to be young forever.

Many cultures have legends of a Fountain of Youth, a spring that reputedly gives endless youth to anyone who drinks its waters. The exploits of Alexander the Great include a tale of a quest for magical healing waters, while other legends tell of the elixir of life, a potion that gives health and everlasting youth. The Spanish explorer Ponce de Leon went in search of the Fountain of Youth in 1513; instead, he discovered Florida.

You can visit the Fountain of Youth National Archaeological Park in St. Augustine, Florida, today and see the site where the Spanish conquistadors first came ashore on April 3, 1513. The spring there has no power to give youth, but that has not stopped people for searching for ways to stay young.

You can find examples in any magazine, where you will see advertisements for creams, vitamins, cosmetics, drinks, and more, all that will supposedly make someone look and feel younger.

Go on your own media quest for the fountain of youth. Grab a friend and a bunch of magazines and newspapers (maybe from your family's recycling bin). Each of you takes a pile and looks through, tearing out all the advertisements for products that are designed to keep people youthful. When you've finished, see who has found the most ads for youth-enhancing products—does the winner look any younger? For bonus points, make a collage of the ads.

160. Write a Persuasive Speech

We all need to be persuasive at some point in all our lives—and usually at many points.

In other words, we need to convince someone else to see things the way we do.

A good speech can move its listeners so much that they change their minds—even on opinions strongly held. Some examples in history include Moses appealing to Pharaoh to free his people or Sir Winston Churchill urging the people of Britain to fight against the Nazis. More recent famous words that you may have heard have been spoken by Martin Luther King, Jr., ("I have a dream,") and John F. Kennedy ("Ask not what your country can do for you...").

How would you write such a plea? Write a speech about something that is important to you. It doesn't have to be on a subject of international importance, but it should be about something that you care about. Does your school cafeteria offer healthy, tasty lunches? Write about why it should. Or perhaps you want a pet—write a speech that tells why you want it and how you would take care of it.

Once you've written your speech, try it out on family and friends and ask them to rate your powers of persuasion on a scale of 1 (meaning not very persuasive) to 5 (superbly persuasive).

161. Draw Pangaea

If you would guess that Pangaea is the crud that accumulates inside cooking pots or a new line of jogging shorts, you'd be a world off.

Pangaea is the supposed "supercontinent" that existed before tectonic activity split it into what became the continents we know today.

Draw Pangaea by imagining our 7 continents smushed together. While you *can* look at maps of the continents today, you *can't* look at artists' renditions of what Pangaea might have looked like.

If you want to simulate Pangaea's breakup, turn the drawing into a puzzle by pasting the sheet onto a piece of cardboard that is the same size, dividing it into puzzle pieces with faint pencil lines, and cutting along the pencil lines.

162. Write a Letter to an Editor

Anyone can get published in the newspaper—you don't have to be a journalist or even an adult.

All you need to do is write a thoughtful letter about a situation affecting your community. You might already have an opinion about something going on in town, and you could use that as the subject of your letter. If nothing comes to mind, read the local paper for a few days to get an idea. Say your town is about to build a new elementary school on a main road. Maybe you'd write that you feel that location is too dangerous. Or what if the main park is planning to ban dogs. Do you agree? Your issue doesn't have to be controversial. Sometimes letters just support a story the paper has already run, adding a new detail to it.

Send off your letter and check the "Letters to the Editor" page in the paper for the next few days. Maybe your letter and name will be there.

163. Coin Jar Head to Head

This game involves spare change and best guesses.

Many families keep a jar near the front door, or on the kitchen counter, for spare change. Ask any friends who belong to such a family to gather together—and bring the jars of change. Everyone who's playing silently estimates how many coins are in each jar and writes their estimate for each jar on individual secret ballots. Then you all roll up your sleeves and count the coins in each of the jars. Keep them separate! And grab some snacks—it could take a while. Remember, you're not adding the amount of money, simply the number of coins, regardless of denomination.

Whoever is closest—or correct—wins. One possible reward could be a pool of money, composed of 100 pennies donated from each jar.

164. Make a Seasonal Meal

We don't dress the same year round, so why should we eat the same?

In the olden days, people ate only foods that were in season. They had no choice—they didn't have stores which could fly in oranges (a winter fruit) during the summer or blueberries (a summer fruit) during the winter. They grew their own food, and nature told them what was in season.

Prepare a meal and dessert using vegetables and fruits that are in season in summer (like broccoli, eggplant, green beans and apricots, nectarines, peaches, and berries). In the process, you'll also be able to support your community's farms—some supermarkets indicate when produce is grown locally.

To add a level of challenge to this activity, prepare a color-coded summertime meal. Simply pick a color (red, for example) and try to build a meal using only red-colored summertime foods. The plates, napkins, and utensils you use can be red too.

After your meal, arrange a visit to a farm to ask the farmer why some foods grow only in certain seasons.

165. Keep a Lookup Log

A lookup log is like a best friend or a tasty snack—something you always want by your side.

A lookup log is a little notebook where you jot down words you come across that pose a most common problem: you don't know what they mean and you can't figure it out from the context. Any time you're about to read anything, first pull out your lookup log. After you visit a dictionary, check off each word you looked up and write a brief definition of the word in your log.

Do this either while you're reading or as soon afterward as possible so you don't forget everything you just read. To sharpen your understanding, try writing a sentence with each word below its definition in your lookup log. Then try out one of your words on your family over dinner to see whether they know the word.

166. Build a Scarecrow

These days, large farms don't have to use scarecrows to frighten off feathered pests.

Some farms use special sonic wave machines that send out noise that is unpleasant to birds. Others hang strips of iridescent foil that flap and crinkle in the breeze and glitter in the sun—signals that birds interpret as danger.

Building a scarecrow is rural retro. But you don't need to have a field to have a scarecrow. You don't even need to have crows! Raid your parents' closet for their most hideous old clothes. Flannel shirts and jeans work especially well. Stuff them with hay or newspaper (or old rags and more clothes) and tie the clothes closed at the waist, wrists, and ankles. Attach the torso to the legs with more string or safety pins. Fill a small burlap sack or old pillowcase with stuffing for the head, and provide a face with permanent marker. Accessorize as you wish, from a hat to boots to braces—then set him outside your door to see who you can creep out besides crows.

167. Compare Card Collections

You can only look at your baseball (or movie, or gaming) card collection so many times.

Here's something different you can do with it. Compare the size of your collection with the collection of a friend who also collects cards—in more than one way.

1. First, who has more cards total? Each count the number of cards you own, including repeats.

2. But who has the most *unique* cards? Count just the number of repeats and subtract from the total to determine who has the greater number of non-repeat cards.

You may find that the person with the larger *number* of cards may actually have fewer *different* cards than the other person.

If you collect something other than cards, from coins to candy bar wrappers, do the same with a friend who also collects the same thing.

168. Odds versus Evens

Odds are even you will like this game.

It's kind of a cross between spin the bottle and tag, but with math. It may sound strange, but this works best with 19 participants. (That's a math challenge right there—rounding up exactly 19 people to play. But hey, we humans can do amazing things if we're determined. Plus it's summer—everyone is looking for something to do, and everyone is at least 19 people.) Each player picks a number between −9 and 9, but no 2 players can pick the same number. Therefore, all 19 numbers (including 0) will be represented. If you don't have 19 players, the number of players with odd numbers should be equal to (or only one off from) the number of evens. Each player writes his number on a sheet of paper and tapes it to the front of his shirt.

All players stand in a circle and someone tosses a stick into the middle. The players at the 2 ends of the stick point to call out their numbers. Everyone mentally adds the 2 numbers in their heads. The person wearing the sum of those 2 numbers must get to the middle before being tagged by anyone else—hopefully she's a fast adder *and* runner! (It's possible no one will have that number. The more players you have, the less likely it is that this will happen. But if it does, just try again.) If tagged, the player is out. Keep repeating until too many people are tagged out to continue.

Here's an example of the game in action: The stick points to 5 and −8. The 2 kids wearing those numbers shout them out with gusto. Whoever is wearing −3 (the sum of those 2 numbers) must bolt to the center before being tagged.

What if the stick points to numbers whose sum is not present? You can just do over or you can play with this fun twist. Say the stick points to 9 and 8. Nobody is wearing the number 17—but one person is wearing 1 and another is wearing 7. So both of them have to run into the middle before being tagged.

169. Clichés Unlimited

See what happens when you use too much of a good thing.

When we write, we sometimes use clichés, which are words or phrases that are heard so often they become shorthand and don't pack as much of an impact as they used to. Some examples are "dead as a doornail" or "the greatest thing since sliced bread." These phrases were once very expressive, but by now they are overused. Good writing is free of clichés, but it can be hard not to use them. Try this trick: write a simple paragraph describing something familiar—and put all the clichés you can think of into it. "I was on cloud nine when I fell head over heels for the new kid on the block. She was fit as a fiddle and pretty as a picture."

170. Guess the Woods

You may know your way around the woods with your eyes closed, but do you know what's *from* the woods with your eyes closed?

Set up a station of objects found in the nearest forest (pine cones, leaves, twigs, soil, moss, bark, and so on) mixed in with things that are not commonly found there (examples could include a seashell, hay, a brick, a banana, or a plastic plant). Blindfold a friend and let him try to figure out what the objects are by touch and smell.

As you gather your objects, if you're in doubt whether something is poisonous, let it be.

171. Write a Press Release

Reporters don't always find news. Sometimes, news finds them.

When companies have news they want the rest of us to know about, they write a press release and send it to newspapers and TV stations.

They hope that a reporter may then write a story about it. A press release has one purpose—to get people excited about the company or something the company has done.

Since you probably don't have a company, you're probably wondering what you could write a press release about. Come up with something worthy of mass attention! Break a world record (just don't break any bones while doing it). Organize a fundraiser for charity, such as a car wash where all proceeds will go toward multiple sclerosis research. Or perhaps one of your parents has a company that could use a press release, so offer to help with that.

Look through your local newspaper. See what kinds of articles are printed about local people. You may get other ideas about what your press release could be about.

Some tips for making your press release required reading:

- A snappy headline (humor usually works)

- A riveting opening sentence (grab their attention right away)

- Stick to the facts (otherwise it's fiction, not news)

- Avoid too many adjectives (use strong verbs instead)

- Keep it to one page (editors are too busy to read more)

- Send it to local (not national) media (you'll have a better shot)

Maybe it will make it into print! Some editors run well-written press releases as is—they don't change a word.

172. Rewrite History Plays

Some of the greatest people in history never heard of some of the other greatest people in history—because some died before others were born.

Pretend that they all lived at the same time, and choose any 2 to star in a mini-play that you'll write and direct. What if Squanto met Rosa Parks? What if the Wright Brothers met Neil Armstrong and the other astronauts who were the first to land on the moon? How about if Cleopatra met Bill Clinton?

You'll want to read up on the accomplishments of the history celebs you choose before you start writing. Beyond that, you'll have to guess how they would react to one another, and have fun with it. There are no wrong answers! Then put on the play for family and friends.

173. "What I Did during School"

At the start of the school year, the cliché first assignment is to write an essay addressing (or even entitled) "What I Did during My Summer Vacation."

Since this book kicks off summer, flip the cliché assignment above on its head—write an essay about what you did during the school year you just finished. Don't bemoan—brainstorm.

Start with the highlights of the year for your essay. It can be a broad essay about a variety of things, or it can focus on one significant event. Say you realized in science class that you want to be a marine biologist. Or perhaps it was the first year you weren't afraid of gym class—and actually scored a couple of goals. The only requirement is that it must be school-related.

When you go back to school in the fall, maybe your teacher will even accept this essay as your first assignment instead of that other topic.

174. Throw a Toga Party

In ancient Rome, nothing said fashion like a sheet—uh, toga.

Roman men wore togas, while the women wore *stolas*. Though they look easy to put on, they were actually heavy garments that were draped and folded in special ways over the body. Made of wool, there were different colors and patterns for togas depending on who you were—most wore white, but the poor wore darker togas and high-ranking government officials wore white with a purple border.

Host a toga and *stola* party in which everyone must come dressed in one—but there's no need to learn the intricate folding and draping methods employed by the ancients. A sheet wrapped around you over your summer clothes and tied so it won't fall off will do just fine.

At the party, have a speed-dressing contest in which participants remove their togas or *stolas*, then race to put it back on before the rest can. Then whoever didn't race can vote on who wears his or her toga or *stola* with the most style.

175. Enjoy the Year's Longest Day

In the Northern Hemisphere, June 21 is the longest day of the year in terms of hours of daylight.

In honor of that, do as much involving the "longest" as you can. Find out what the longest common word in the English language is. Eat the longest piece of food you can think of. Run the longest distance you're capable of. Strike a pose and hold it for the longest amount of time possible. You'll come up with more—surely you're long on ideas!

Also do some amateur detective work to dig up a few facts about the longest things on Earth—for starters, the longest river, the longest animal, and the longest peninsula.

176. Water from Where?

What, you think the water you drink just falls from the sky?

Okay, it does. But it doesn't fall directly into your mouth—it goes through many other channels first. And you often can't tell just by looking at it how pure it is.

Call your local water company to find out if your faucet delivers reservoir water (public/municipal water) or well water (private water, which is pumped and sometimes filtered from soil). Public water is regulated by the government, but private water isn't. Also call your town's health department or environmental services department to find out how to test your drinking water. They might have a kit you can pick up and use. The quality of the drinking water will be determined by the levels of chemicals such as fluoride and chloride it contains as compared to Environmental Protection Agency standards. Does your water measure up? If not, join forces with an adult to let your town know their water purification needs a wake-up call.

While we're wondering about water, consider this. Some people think bottled water is automatically cleaner than tap water. Your bottled water may have a remote mountain stream on its label, but that isn't necessarily the real source. It's usually easier to find out exactly where your tap water comes from. If you can't easily track down a bottled water source to test it, at least test the taste—and compare with your local liquid. Ask a sibling or friend to pour a glass of tap water and a glass of bottled water while you look away. Make sure she remembers which glass is which. Sip both. Can you tell?

177. Make an Unfold Formula

Test your math—and your luck.

Play this game with a group of friends. The first player folds a piece of paper over once, then writes one part of a formula (for example, "3 +") on the folded section facing up. The next person folds the paper again and writes another part of a formula (say, "20 –") on the paper.

Continue until the paper can't be folded anymore, at which point the person to get the paper must solve the formula—and everyone else must check his math. No one may use any numbers with more than 2 digits. This game can be played with 2 or more people, since the players can just alternate writing until the end of the folding. If you create a formula that doesn't work, just try again until you get one that does.

178. Add an Epilogue to a Book

As you read a good book, the question constantly on your mind is probably "What comes next?"

Normally you should develop your own characters when writing your own stories, but allow yourself to make an exception.

Choose a book you like that doesn't end with an epilogue—and write your own. An epilogue is typically a brief concluding chapter after the last one that ties up any loose ends or just revisits the characters a bit in the future for one more scene. You can write your epilogue in any way that comes to mind, but make sure it ties into the plot of the book and try to write it in the same style. An epilogue can even hint at the next story, if there will be one.

211

179. Investigate a River's Youth

Like people, rivers were once young, though unlike people, they didn't often ask for a raise in their allowances.

Use your town's library or historical society to trace the path of a nearby river or stream. Was it in the same place 100 years ago? What about 200 years ago? Are the banks natural or partly man-made (meaning composed of landfill)?

If the river has changed course, get a current map of your town and draw in the position of how the river used to look at some point in the town's history. Continue the detective work by finding out what types of buildings or structures sat along the river in the past—perhaps a mill or a dock—and see if any remnants of any of them are still standing today.

180. Table of Contents versus Index

Here's a fight in which no one can possibly get hurt.

At either end of many nonfiction books, there is a resource to guide you through the middle. In front, it's the table of contents, which lists the information in the book in the order in which it appears, usually by chapters. In back, it's the index, which lists the information alphabetically.

Find a book that has both a table of contents and an index and compare the usefulness of each. Does one help you find information in the book quicker than the other? Also, test the index by using it in the reverse way: as you read the book and come across a subject, see if it is indexed. If you are reading a book about ancient Rome and come to a section on gladiators, you'll definitely find "gladiator" in the index. But will you find, say, the specific types of gladiators (Thracian, Samnite, murmillo, laquearius) listed individually?

181. Three Rocks, One Search

What's harder than rocks? Finding rocks. Specifically, finding specific kinds of rocks.

The world is full of rocks. They may all seem the same, but there are actually 3 main types of the natural nuggets—sedimentary, igneous, and metamorphic. Within each of those categories are many examples of specific kinds of rocks. You can be a rock hunter.

Here are power pairs for each:

Sedimentary

- Shale
- Limestone

Metamorphic

- Slate
- Marble

Igneous

- Granite
- Basalt

Sedimentary rocks often feel gritty and can look like various rocks fused together. This is because they *are* various rocks fused together.

Igneous rocks look like crystals. They form when magma cools.

Metamorphic rocks usually form underground by extreme heat and may look more uniform.

Find out what types exist in your area. One way to do this is to check the maps on the Wikipedia Web site.

Another is to contact the U.S. Geological Survey or check out the USGS Web site, or call any local rock enthusiasts' association.

If you have more than one type in your region, make a list of the types and look at photos in books or online. Then go on a scavenger hunt for as many types as you can dig up. Start a jar for each of the 3 types and drop in new rocks as you come across them.

182. We're All Animals

Are you a monkey or a rooster? Is your brother a goat?

According to Chinese tradition, each year is represented by one of 12 animals. For example, 2006 is the year of the dog and 2007 is the year of the pig.

Find out what animal goes with the years in which each member of your family was born. Make each family member a poster or collage related to that animal. You can even set up a radio to play the sounds of that animal as they walk out one morning.

Also, find out *why* the Chinese began to use animals to represent years and *how* they chose these 12 particular animals. When you do, you can use that information to quiz your family on the years of the 12 animals over Chinese food. Throw in a few animals that aren't part of the Chinese zodiac—such as cats and wolves—and see if they notice.

183. Blueprint Your Block

Maps represent the distance of things on Earth—proportionately.

In other words, a mile on the planet may equal an inch on paper. Measure the distance between several houses on your block; if you're a city kid, you can do the same with apartment building entrances.

Create a blueprint of your street using proportions (100 feet equals 1 inch, for example, since miles probably don't apply!). Include other things, too,

like big trees, mailboxes, jungle gyms, or any other significant structures. Draw each item from a bird's-eye view, the way architectural plans look.

By making a proportion key, you can blueprint anything, even small areas such as a backyard or even your room.

184. Write Your Own Greeting Cards

Summer birthdays can be bummers.

Let's face it, some of the best—and biggest—parties happen in school. And because kids are away on vacations or at camp in the summer, they may forget that a friend back home is turning a year older.

Make up for that by making a birthday card for a friend whose birthday falls in June, July, or August. In a store, look at greeting cards to get ideas and see how they use humor. A card doesn't need humor, of course, but everyone likes to laugh! Make your card by hand or use a computer. Either way, your friend will appreciate your personal touch. A successful card connects with a person's emotions in some way, and makes the person feel good (even if it teases him too).

185. Make Your Own Compost

In order to grow beautiful flowers and tasty vegetables, gardens need compost—decaying plant life that's super-nutritious.

Luckily, compost is easy to make. Choose a spot in your backyard for your compost pile; be sure your parents approve of the location. Dig a shallow hole. Then add a mixture of branches, wood chips, and leaves (these things contain lots of carbon) plus grass, weeds, and maybe some manure (these things contain lots of nitrogen). Sprinkle with water so your compost pile is evenly moist and add some air by turning over the contents of the pile with a rake.

Now, let nature do its magic. Your compost pile will attract bacteria, insects, and worms that will feed on it. Turn over your compost regularly so it gets enough air and keep it moist. When you turn it, you'll notice that it's steamy and hot; that shows that the bacteria are hard at work.

Over time, critters will break down your compost into super-rich food for you garden. Be patient, it could take all summer for it to be ready. When your compost smells rich and earthy and has broken down into such tiny bits you can't recognize any branches or leaves or wood chips in it, it's time to feed your plants. Add a little compost to your houseplants and spread some around your family's garden. If plants could talk, they'd thank you!

186. Keep a Cloud Journal

Are you the type of person who walks around with your head in the clouds, spotting fluffy white sheep and other critters in the sky?

If so, why not keep a cloud journal where you can track all of your cloud sightings and observations. Choose a small, unlined notebook and tie a pencil with a string to it so you can carry your journal with you where ever you go.

In the first pages of your journal, you should create a miniature field guide to clouds to help you identify the clouds you spot. First, make notes about the 3 main types of clouds: cirrus, cumulus, and stratus.

Describe each type, draw a picture, and explain what type of weather each cloud brings. You should also add entries for cumulonimbus clouds (these are what you call cumulus clouds that produce rain or snow) and stratocumulus (combination stratus and cumulus clouds) in case you spot these varieties.

Other possible entries to include are contrail, the ice crystals that trail behind jets in thin, white lines. (The term is a combination of "condensation" and "trail.")

Cirrocumulus is another type of cloud made from ice crystals rather than water droplets; add an entry and draw a picture of this cloud type too.

Once you've completed your mini field guide, you are ready to start spotting and logging clouds of your own. For each entry, write down the date, then note the kind of cloud you spot, draw a picture, and make a prediction about tomorrow's weather, if you can. Note in your journal whether your weather prediction was correct or incorrect. If you were wrong about the weather, look at your journal again and see if you might have incorrectly identified the clouds you saw.

If you spot a flying saucer–shaped cloud, or another type of cloud that you can't find in your field guide, write a thorough description of it in your journal, draw a picture, and note what the weather was like when you spotted it. Then do some research at the library or online to figure out what your "mystery cloud" might be.

187. Plot a Neolithic Revolution

You may be surprised to learn that people didn't always farm.

Sometime during the Neolithic Revolution (circa 9,000 to 6,000 B.C.E. in Asia), early humans switched from a nomadic, hunter-gatherer way of life to a sedentary, agricultural way of life. Some scholars consider that the most significant change in human history. But what smaller changes might this have caused in terms of the everyday life of those people? They couldn't exactly go to a garden center and buy seeds or to a hardware store for tools.

Imagine that your family has time traveled back to Neolithic times. Write a short story about what changes your mom, dad, and siblings might face as they transition from hunters who roamed for prey to farmers who stayed in one place. What might your average dinner look like, before and after this change?

188. Write Beginnings and Endings

Some people believe that the first line of a book is the most important. Others think that the last line is the key.

You're going to write both—but not the story in between!

A story prompt is the first line or first few lines of a story. Usually story prompts are exciting, mysterious, or funny, and they end in a cliffhanger—indicated by the 3 dots called an *ellipsis*. Here's an example of a story prompt: "After school I walk home with my next-door neighbor Miles. It's been the same every day all year. Until yesterday. As we got to his house,

sitting in the front yard was a . . ." You see how that could go in any direction?

Write a story prompt of your own. Also, write one story prompt that is the *end*, not the beginning, of a story. The challenge would then be to write whatever happened to lead up to that dramatic ending.

When you're done, share your prompts with friends and see what their imaginations can do with them.

No, that's not a big boat that holds 2 of each character.

This is arc with a "c"—meaning a curved path.

After reading a book, identify how the main character changes from the beginning to the end. On a sheet of paper, draw a large arc—it is simply a line that looks like the setting sun over the horizon (but without the horizon). The left side of the arc represents the character at the beginning of the story and the right side represents him at the end.

Along the arc, write a short observation about the character at each stage (or in each chapter) of the story. This can be about the character's actions or beliefs, which may change often or may change only once. When you notice that the character has changed in some way, also write what you think caused the change.

190. Create a Feel-Good Memorial

Many memorials commemorate tragic events: wars, natural disasters, and other kinds of loss. But memorials can keep happy memories alive, too.

In fact, memorials can be built to celebrate any event that is significant to the society that creates it, such as an important scientific discovery, an athletic achievement, or an artistic accomplishment.

Why not preserve a little bit of happiness and create a memorial that celebrates a notable event in the life of your family? You could mark the birth of a new sibling, a wedding, or even a great family vacation that brought everyone together for a good time. Any happy event that is significant to you and your family will do.

Don't think that you have to chisel a sculpture out of marble, or build a tower. Your memorial can be a collage made out of cardboard and photographs, or a diorama built with figurines and other miniatures, or even a Web site. The idea is to create a tribute that will remind your family members of a happy event every time they look at it.

191. Question the First Chapter

The first chapter of a book needs to have enough going on to hook you.

At the same time, it can't have so much going on that you're overwhelmed—and it should never give too much away.

Choose a book to read. After finishing the first chapter, write any questions you have that it raises but doesn't answer. Then put them away and keep reading, straight to the finish.

When you're done with the book, revisit your list and see how many of your questions were eventually answered and how many are still mysteries. Do you like when everything is tied up, or do you not mind a few loose ends?

192. Lemonade Stand Face-off

Forget air-conditioning. What we need to make summer cooler is more lemonade stands.

You and a friend open lemonade stands with the exact same materials and on the same day—but in different neighborhoods. You don't need to be far away; it can simply be 2 parallel streets. You're competing to see who can make the most money in a day. While part of the winner's success will probably depend on location, part will be based on sales and marketing.

Here's the math part: at one stand, advertise 3 cups for 1 dollar (roughly 33 cents each) and at the other, offer cups at 50 cents each. See which sells better and who makes more money at the end of the day.

193. Ready, Set, Boil

You already know that water boils at 212°F (100°C). But what happens if salted water, dried pasta, and plain old water race to the boiling point?

Before you set up this experiment in your kitchen, be sure to ask for your parents' permission. To make the race fair, you'll need three pots of equal size filled with equal amounts of water (use a measuring cup). You'll also want the following tools on hand: a kitchen thermometer, a stopwatch or watch with a second hand, and a log to record the losers and the winner.

Put each of the pots on a separate burner, then add 3 tablespoons salt to one of the pots and 1 cup pasta to another pot. Don't add anything but the water to the third pot. Turn each of the burners to medium-high and start watching your watch.

The first pot to show bubbles that break the surface of the water wins the boiling race. Record how long it took and also record the temperature of the winning pot. Then wait to see which pot comes in second and third, recording time and temperature for each.

Does adding ingredients to water shorten or lengthen the time that it takes to bring the water to a boil? If you need more time to ponder this question, do it while you wait for the pasta to finish cooking (it should take 8 to 10 minutes), then enjoy it with a little salt and some butter.

194. Map Your Town 100 Years Ago

A century ago, your town was probably crisscrossed by dirt roads and teeming with horse-drawn carriages.

Head to the local library and historical center to discover what else was in your town back then. They surely have photos and documents that will bring the past to life.

Then create an "old-time" map of your town; if that's too big a task, focus on just your neighborhood or even your street. Include sidebars of facts about any interesting people of that era that you come across. Any buildings from then that are still standing today? Draw a special symbol on them and indicate in a key what that symbol means.

195. Index a Fiction Book

You're probably thinking that indexes are for nonfiction books only. Says who?

How many times have you been reading a story and you come upon a detail that makes you want to go back and reread a particular passage—only you don't remember where that is? Or you come across a character who has been mentioned once before, but you have no idea where or in what context he first appeared? It's frustrating to flip back and spend minutes and minutes searching.

Take a book you know inside and out and create an index for it. Make note of every appearance of every character, major or not. (For a major one, an entry may look like this: "Protagonist, Jill, 1-296."

For a minor one: "Cameo, Fred, 37.") Also include key "props" if there are any, such as an old car or an invisibility cloak, and other details such as locations and references to real-world events such as Independence Day, the first moon landing, or whatever the case may be.

You can even index key scenes, such as "Jill meets Jack for the first time"—though that could take a while! As for format, simply model it after any other index you've seen—list the entries alphabetically and make it as detailed as possible.

196. Food Group Survey

When it comes to eating, everyone has something to say.

Poll 50 people (relatives, friends, friends of friends, parents of friends, classmates, neighbors, your mail carrier, the cashiers at the supermarket, and anyone else you can think of) with a simple question: What is your favorite food? It has to be a real food with nutritional value—no junk food such as candy, cookies, chips, or ice cream allowed!

Graph the results by food group and see what percentage of people named a food from dairy, grains, fruits, vegetables, and meats/eggs/nuts. Which percentage is most/least popular?

Then gather together the 5 most common responses—or, if there aren't enough duplicates, your 5 personal favorites out of all responses—and conduct a smaller survey. Gather a small group of family or friends and have a blind taste test of those 5 foods. One food will emerge as the ultimate favorite.

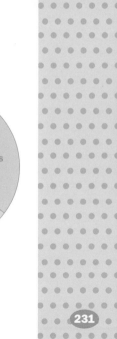

Fruit 10%
Vegetables 20%
Grains 24%
Meats/Nuts/Eggs 23%
Dairy 23%

By now, that poor donkey is pretty sore.

So try this less painful variation of "Pin the Tail on the Donkey." Instead of pinning tails on animals, you'll be sticking former names of cities or countries onto the current names of those cities or countries.

Get as large a world map as you can, either from *National Geographic*, a store, or the Internet; alternatively, you can sketch one yourself. On small labels, write the ancient names of modern cities. Use this list, but don't write the modern names (they're here only to give you an advantage!):

Babylon (now Iraq)

Byzantium (Istanbul)

Constantinople (Istanbul)

Carthage (Tunis, Tunisia)

Gaul (France and Belgium)

Halicarnassus (Bodrum, Turkey)

Mesopotamia (Iraq)

Persia (Iran)

Phoenicia (Syria and Lebanon)

Sumer (Iraq)

Troy (Turkey)

Judea (Israel)

Peking (Beijing)

Leningrad (St. Petersburg)

Search for more if you'd like. Then try to stick each ancient city over its modern counterpart on the map. No blindfold is needed to play—this game is hard enough already!

198. Read Your Young(er) Writing

No matter what kind of lives we go on to have as adults, we all have one thing in common as kids—we all write.

In school, that takes many forms. Surely your parents have saved your first attempts at everything—writing a story, writing an essay, writing *period*.

Revisit your past and see what the world looked like through your younger eyes. You may be amused to see what you spelled wrong—and impressed to see what you spelled right. You may also rediscover the innocence of the beginning writer.

If you find a piece of your writing that is inspirational in some way, hang it over your desk. It will make you smile and also remind you how far you've come.

199. Make Instructions Clearer

Quizzes have them. Assembly-required furniture has them. Pasta packages have them. Sometimes notes left on the kitchen table from Mom or Dad have them.

We're talking about instructions. Have you ever read instructions that didn't seem to make sense?

If you can eventually figure them out, try to rewrite them more clearly, either for you in the future or for someone else. This could be instructions on how to get somewhere (a.k.a. directions), how to install software, how to put together a toy ("some aggravating assembly required"), how to solve a certain type of math problem, and so on. You'll be helping to make life a little less confusing.

200. The Year That Was

Every December, magazines look back at the year that's about to end.

Magazines didn't always exist, so make up for a past year that didn't get a glossy retrospective treatment. Choose a year between 1000 and 1800. Using books and sites, find out what the key events of that year were in the Eastern Hemisphere (Europe, Africa, Asia, Australia).

Design a magazine-style "year-end wrap-up" cover for your chosen year, making it the same size as a standard magazine. Refer to any of *Time* and *Newsweek's* recent annual year-end issues for ideas. They'll be available in your local library.

On your cover, include a few teasing headlines about the year's big stories and either a full-page image or a collage of images representative of that year. Then slip your fake cover over a real mag and leave it on the coffee table. Have fun watching how family and guests react.

Subject Checklist

Math

Reading

Science

Social Studies